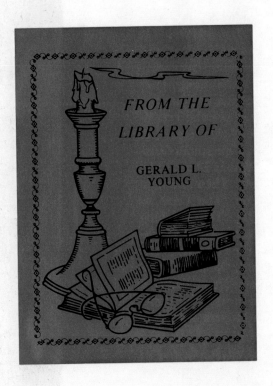

THE CROSS OF CHRIST

THE CROSS OF CHRIST

Eight Public Lectures

BY

VINCENT TAYLOR
D.D., F.B.A.

LONDON
MACMILLAN & CO LTD
NEW YORK · ST MARTIN'S PRESS
1957

MACMILLAN AND COMPANY LIMITED
London Bombay Calcutta Madras Melbourne

THE MACMILLAN COMPANY OF CANADA LIMITED
Toronto

ST MARTIN'S PRESS INC
New York

PRINTED IN GREAT BRITAIN

PREFACE

THESE chapters consist of eight Public Lectures delivered at Drew University, Madison, New Jersey, U.S.A., in the Fall Semester of 1955–6, to an audience consisting of professors, students, preachers, and members of the general public, and they are here presented very much in the form in which they were first spoken. To address an audience of this kind is not easy if one seeks both to sustain interest and at the same time to deal fully with New Testament teaching. The reader is therefore invited to estimate them in the light of the circumstances in which they were first composed and delivered

Although I have previously treated the doctrine of the Atonement in *Jesus and His Sacrifice* (1937), *The Atonement in New Testament Teaching* (1940), and *Forgiveness and Reconciliation* (1941), these Lectures are an independent attempt to set forth its meaning. I think that theologians ought not to be in bondage to what they have already written, but should strive repeatedly to express themselves more adequately, seeking, in the words of Solon, to grow older learning every day.

The Lectures are based on the New Testament, for I hold that the Scriptures are the primary source of Christian doctrine, a view which is accepted in every part of the Christian Church. In interpreting the Bible we must apply the principles of textual, literary, and historical criticism, but the use of these methods is by no means inconsistent with the belief that Scripture is the medium of divine revelation. This conviction is sustained by the remarkable unity of Biblical teaching, the progressive character of the revelation it contains, its abiding power in the life of the Church and in the experience of individual believers, and its place and influence in world history. No other writings stand on the same plane. The basis for authority for Christian belief and practice is, in my view, the testimony of Scripture, the historic witness of the Church, and the illumination of the Holy Spirit.

I take the opportunity of expressing my indebtedness to those who attended the Lectures at Drew and to the sympathy and support of Dean Stanley R. Hopper, Dean Bernhard W. Anderson, Professor John Paterson, and Professor Geoffrey W. Stafford, who took it in turn to preside.

I am much indebted to the Editors of *The Expository Times* who permitted me to draw upon an article in Vol. xlviii, 267–73, on ' The Best Books on the Atonement ' in Lecture 7, and to my friend and former student, the Rev. W. F. Hewitson, B.A., B.D., for his help in the correction of the proofs. I trust these Lectures may prove to be of value to those readers who desire a brief statement of the Biblical basis of the doctrine of the Atonement and a constructive account of its meaning for today.

VINCENT TAYLOR

CONTENTS

		PAGE
PREFACE		V
1. THE CROSS AS ETERNAL AND AS AN EVENT IN TIME		I
2. THE CROSS AS JESUS HIMSELF SAW IT		II
3. THE TEACHING OF ST. PAUL (i) THE MEANING OF THE CROSS		24
4. THE TEACHING OF ST. PAUL (ii) THE CROSS IN CHRISTIAN EXPERIENCE		35
5. THE TEACHING OF THE EPISTLE TO THE HEBREWS		50
6. THE TEACHING OF ST. JOHN		60
7. MODERN THEORIES OF THE ATONEMENT		71
8. TOWARDS A MODERN STATEMENT OF THE DOCTRINE		87
INDEX OF SCRIPTURE QUOTATIONS		105

I

THE CROSS AS ETERNAL AND AS AN EVENT IN TIME

EVERY reader of the Markan Passion Narrative is impressed by the precision with which the Evangelist speaks of the times when the tragic events happened. He mentions the third, the sixth, and the ninth hours. Of the Crucifixion he says, 'And it was the third hour, and they crucified him' (Mk. xv. 25). This precision is striking when we consider the eternal significance which the writer of the Epistle to the Hebrews finds in the death of Christ in the words, 'But he, when he had offered one sacrifice for sins for ever, sat down on the right hand of God' (Heb. x. 12).

How, we ask, can an event which took place during an afternoon in A.D. 29 or 30 be of decisive importance for the Christian of today? With Lessing, the philosopher asks how the accidental truths of history can be evidence for the necessary truths of reason. The plain man says, 'Is not the Crucifixion a distant event, dead and done with?' It is evident that in this matter a great religious interest is at stake. We are bound to consider how we think of time, whether past events are only isolated points in a series, or whether God invades history with abiding consequences. This issue seriously engages the attention of theologians today. It is best considered by reflecting upon (1) Events as Points in the Time-Series; (2) Events with Permanent Significance; and (3) Events as Divine Invasions in Time.

I. EVENTS AS POINTS IN THE TIME SERIES

As we look back many events which must have happened seem to be dead fixed points. To use a simile with which Oscar Cullmann has made us familiar, they look like dots on a rising line, bisected by the present into past and future. Things of yesterday, we say, are isolated pegs on the clothes line of Time.

There is much to support this opinion. We look back through the mists of time and recall events which must have happened. We may think of Caractacus trying out his new chariot, of Boadicea completing her toilet by the use of a burnished Roman mirror, of some ancient Briton fishing not far from the shore in his coracle, of an ancient Saxon farmer tilling common land, of the landing on the coast of England of some Norse raider, of American pioneers journeying out into the unknown. All these things happened, but they have passed like the snowflakes of yesterday.

Robert Burns has given us an immortal picture of country life in his description of the cotter's Saturday night, and Thomas Gray in his *Elegy* has described the mute inglorious life of simple men and women.

> 'Along the cool sequester'd vale of life
> They kept the noiseless tenor of their way.'

We think of many single events known to us by experience or by reading: a face seen in passing, a country fair, a blow struck, a person met, the daily life of a buried city, the quiet life of some ancient monastery. 'Ships that pass in the night' has become a common and familiar phrase. These events are past and gone; they stirred the pool of life for a while; but now the rings have ceased to spread and all is calm. The words of Ecclesiasticus xliv, so often read in these post-War years, bring home to us in all its poignancy the transience of human life and its affairs.

> 'And some there be, which have no memorial;
> Who are perished as though they had not been.'

The Crucifixion can be viewed in this manner, as a point in the course of time, a fact of history which belongs to the past. Experts differ about the year in which it happened, most of them fixing upon A.D. 29 or 30. At the Passover season, in the spring of one of these years, the Cross was set up on Golgotha and the nails were driven home. Incomparable as the story really is, it seems a far off event like other ancient tragedies, and one may well ask what is its present meaning. Even when isolated, it stands out as a unique event, if it be true that this Jesus of Nazareth was in truth the Son of God. But more than nineteen centuries have rolled by since it happened. Can it have abiding significance? That is the question we are compelled to ask.

II. EVENTS WITH PERMANENT SIGNIFICANCE

In some of the events already mentioned, apart even from the Cross, we can see a permanent meaning.

The ancient Briton in his coracle stands at the beginning of a long line of development in which the stateliest liner stands at the end. The simplest annals of the poor, told by the poets, have proved to be the foundations of national character. We speak of 'decisive battles of the world', Marathon, Waterloo, the Marne, Alamein, which so far as we can see have changed the course of history. In 1215 on the island of Runnymede, two miles west of Staines, king John took up his pen and signed Magna Carta. It is a past event, and yet Hallam describes this document as 'the keystone of English liberty'. Nay more, it is the basis of democratic freedom the world over. On the thirty-first of October, 1517, Martin Luther might have been seen walking down the streets of Wittenburg and nailing his ninety-five theses on the door of his church. As an event it is dead and gone, but its results live in every part of the world. On Plymouth Hoe there is a stone which bears the simple date 1620, that and nothing more. But from that spot the 'Mayflower' sailed, a tiny vessel as ships go today, yet it was the harbinger of many events in the history of the United States. From 1745 onwards John Wesley might have been seen riding on his horse on his amazing evangelistic tours through the counties of England. These events are 'points upon a line', and yet out of them there has emerged a Church which in its branches numbers millions. In Scottish religious history there are few more thrilling events than those connected with 'the Disruption', especially that day on the eighteenth of May, 1843, when Dr. Chalmers, Dr. Cunningham, and Dr. Candlish led from St. Giles that procession of men who left the Church of Scotland for conscience' sake. All of them are gone, yet being dead they still speak. They founded a great Free Church whose members in 1929 united again with their brethren to form the existing Church of Scotland, with its churches, colleges, and missionaries in every part of the earth.

All the isolated events I have mentioned have had abiding results. On a transcendent scale the same is true of the Cross. Christ died, and in the dramatic words of St. Mark Joseph of Arimathaea 'rolled a stone against the door of the tomb' (Mk. xv. 46). The soldiers, the malefactors, and the priests are all dead. As it must have seemed to Caiaphas the 'incident' was closed! But it was far from being ended, and it is not ended yet.

The stone was rolled away and the Easter faith was born,
'Christ is risen'.   His coming into the world has proved
to be the dividing point of history.   His death and
resurrection mark the birth of the Christian Church.
The event is seen to be the inspiration of art and of music,
and in it men have found the soul's living way to God.
Great national shrines reveal the faith of the past and
living churches throughout the world worship the Exalted
Lord.   National barriers have been overcome and social
evils have been exposed and redressed.   Great tasks
remain, especially the problems of war and peace, but
the hope of the world centres in Christ and His Cross.
No other event has had such consequences or contains
within itself such promise for mankind.

These permanent results are a vital part of the answer
to the question, 'Is not the Crucifixion a distant event?',
but they are only a partial answer.   We have still to
consider what it is which gives it eternal significance.   If
we are content to classify Christ's death with other events
of abiding moment, we suggest that while it is sublime,
it is not otherwise essentially different in kind.   The
death of Socrates has had far-reaching results, even if they
are less conspicuous and less profound than those which
have sprung from the death of Jesus.   We need a richer
conception of events if we are to see the supreme spiritual
significance of the Cross.

III. EVENTS AS DIVINE INVASIONS IN THE WORLD OF TIME

There is deep suggestiveness in the way that some
modern scientists speak of 'Emergent Evolution'.   Professor C. Lloyd Morgan used this phrase in his *Emergence
of Novelty*.   The idea suggested by the term is that
Evolution is not simply a matter of steady progress by

slow and gradual variations, but that at points in the age-long process something new has 'emerged' which thence-forward has affected everything. Whether this view is sound must be left to the discussions of scientists and philosophers. It is certainly a matter of the greatest interest that it has a marked religious counterpart.

The student of religious history is often led to think that there are times when, as it seems, God 'makes bare His arm' and puts forth His power to save. Frequently he is inclined to say with the prophet, 'Verily thou art a God that hidest thyself, O God of Israel, the Saviour' (Isa. xlv. 15), and he will exercise a wise reserve when men too readily see in history the finger of God. But there are at least two events in the history of Israel in which it is difficult not to find signs of the emergent activity of God. The first is the Exodus of Israel from Egypt. Deep in the consciousness of the Hebrews lies the convic-tion of divine deliverance, and it is expressed in the words, 'We were Pharaoh's bondmen in Egypt; and the Lord brought us out of Egypt with a mighty hand' (Deuter-onomy vi. 21). The second of these events is the Return from the Babylonian Exile. In the view of the prophets this event was God's doing, a stupendous sign of His mercy and loving-kindness. This strong conviction is voiced in such words as, 'Go you forth from Babylon, flee you from the Chaldeans; with a voice of singing declare you, tell this, utter it even unto the end of the earth: say you, The Lord hath redeemed his servant Jacob' (Isa. xlviii. 20), and it finds expression in the more familiar words, 'Comfort you, comfort you my people, saith your God. Speak you to the heart of Jerusalem, and cry unto her, that her time of service is accomplished, that her iniquity is pardoned; that she hath received of the Lord's hand double for all her sins' (Isa. xl. 1f.).

This way of thinking of the presence of God in history is a religious judgement; its truth cannot be demonstrated so that we are compelled to accept it as historical fact. Our recognition of it depends on whether we believe in God and on how we conceive His activity. It is not the conception of an 'absentee God', who breaks into the course of history only now and then in startling and miraculous deeds, but otherwise dwells apart. It is the view that He who is speaking continuously in sun and in star, in nature and in man, in prophets and poets speaks and acts decisively at the times of His appointing, and challenges us in action so that we must answer 'Yea' or 'Nay'. It is revelation in act and deed. It is the emergence of a reality which is always there.

Now it is from this standpoint that we interpret best the fact of Christ, His life, death, and resurrection. This is precisely what the great New Testament writers do. They begin with the activity of the living God. 'God commends his own love toward us', writes St. Paul, 'in that, while we were yet sinners, Christ died for us' (Rom. v. 8). 'God', says the writer of Hebrews at the very beginning of his Epistle, 'having of old time spoken unto the fathers in the prophets by divers portions and in divers manners, hath at the end of these days spoken unto us in his Son' (Heb. i. 1f.). 'God so loved the world', writes St. John, 'that he gave his only begotten Son, that whosoever believes on him should not perish, but have eternal life' (Jn. iii. 16). And not only does each one begin with God, all of them in various ways go on to speak of a continuous ministry of Christ for men on high (Rom. viii. 34, Heb. i. 3, ix. 24, &c., I Jn. ii. 1f.). In the person and work of Christ the grace of God takes fire and burns undiminished eternally. Such is the teaching of the New Testament.

In modern times no one has expressed this truth more decisively than Professor Oscar Cullmann in his book *Christus und Zeit*, translated into English in *Christ and Time* (1950). Cullmann has shown that time and history find their centre-point in Christ. In Christ God has bisected the line of time, so that all that goes before Him is preparation and all that follows is consequence. The coming of Christ is D-Day; V-Day has yet to come. This statement is a penetrating insight, although the basis of the idea is as old as St. Paul when he says that it was 'in the fulness of the time' that God sent forth His Son, born of a woman, born under the law (Gal. iv. 4). There is nothing accidental in the coming of Christ, but something purposeful and determinative. This coming is like a voice in a series of caves, which draws other sounds into itself, and echoes and reverberates through all the distant galleries of time. Meaning is given to all that is past, to human longing, suffering, and sacrifice, and meaning is provided for all that is to come, so that men who never saw Christ can find in Him the way to fulness of life. With the truest insight St. John presents the significance of Christ in the words, 'And I, if I be lifted up from the earth, will draw all men unto myself' (Jn. xii. 32).

In answer, then, to the question raised at the outset we must say that, while the Cross is an event in history, it is not an isolated event, nor only an event with abiding consequences, but also the invasion of God into human history for the saving and blessing of men. As such, it neither began in A.D. 29 or 30 nor ended then. At that point the love of God emerged and is of vital moment. One recalls the words of Horace Bushnell: 'Nay, there is a cross in God before the wood is seen upon Calvary; hid in God's own virtue itself'. In New

Testament words the truth is best expressed in 2 Cor. v. 19, 'In Christ God was reconciling the world to himself', combined with Heb. ix. 24, where Christ is said to have entered into heaven itself 'now to appear before the face of God for us'.

IV. CONSEQUENCES

Seen in its true perspective the greatness of the Gospel shines in its own light. We do not offer to men a story of the kind which begins, 'Once upon a time nineteen centuries ago', and ends in that age, but the good news of an act of God which is eternally valid; not a saga, but a song still sung, and destined to be sung through all eternity.

> 'Worthy is the Lamb that hath been slain
> To receive the power, and riches, and wisdom,
> And might, and honour, and glory, and blessing.'

We see also its abiding wonder.

The temper of our age is often one of fear, in danger of relapsing into pessimism. The words of H. G. Wells often find an echo in men's hearts: 'The experiment will be over, the crystals gone dissolving down the wastepipe'. How different is the spirit of St. Paul: 'Who shall separate us from the love of Christ? . . . I am persuaded, that neither death, nor life, nor angels, nor principalities, nor things present, nor things to come, nor powers, nor height, nor depth, nor any other creature, shall be able to separate us from the love of God, which is in Christ Jesus our Lord' (Rom. viii. 35–9)! But it is not of safety only that he speaks. 'All things', he writes, 'are yours; whether Paul, or Apollos, or Cephas, or the world, or life, or death, or things present, or things to come; all are yours; and you are Christ's; and Christ is God's' (I Cor. iii. 21–3).

B

These blessings come to us in Christ and His Cross; and it is the meaning of that Cross that we are to study in these lectures: its meaning as Christ saw it, as the great New Testament writers interpreted it, and as, although always in part, we may see it today.

II

THE CROSS AS JESUS HIMSELF
SAW IT

To attempt to say how Jesus interpreted His death is an ambitious inquiry. No apology is needed if it is accomplished only in part. Our sources in the Gospels are limited in extent and open to debate at almost every point, and our ability to trace the thought of the historical Jesus is severely circumscribed. It is not surprising that in many discussions of the doctrine little space is given to this question, and one can understand why many scholars doubt whether positive results can be gained. Bultmann's *Theology of the New Testament*, for example, opens with a brief discussion of the Messianic consciousness of Jesus, which is mainly negative, and then passes on to discuss in detail the theology of the Primitive Church and that of the great New Testament writers. This doubt seems to me excessive. It is hard to believe that Jesus went to His death without any idea of its meaning for Himself and His ministry, and that no glimmer of light breaks through the primitive sources at our disposal. For my own part I believe the Gospels give trustworthy information about His thoughts, provided we do not make impossible demands upon them and are willing to subject them to historical criticism.

In addition to the sources several generations of concentrated study have greatly increased our knowledge of the history of the period and of contemporary religious thought, both Jewish and Greek. In particular, we have learnt much about current Messianic ideas, the concept of the Son of Man, the doctrine of the Suffering Servant, the Temple cultus, and Jewish sacrificial beliefs. The gap between the Old Testament and the New has been narrowed, and through Strack and Billerbeck's invaluable '*Kommentar*'[1] much knowledge has been gained of rabbinical teaching, which, although later than our period, has a long history behind it. Many important articles in Kittel's *Theologisches Wörterbuch*[2] have greatly increased our knowledge of biblical words and conceptions, and we have at our disposal very many learned works and commentaries.[3] We are able to learn much from the mistakes of the past as well as from its achievements, and especially from writers who do not convince us. It is not too much to say that after long periods of digging and sowing, the fields are white unto harvest, and I hope it is not too optimistic to say that in the next decades historical criticism ought to be more constructive than it has been for a long time.

In this lecture I propose to discuss, first, some of the preliminary questions which call for notice, and secondly, with a due appreciation of its difficulty, the question how Jesus interpreted His death.

I. PRELIMINARY QUESTIONS

1. One of these issues is the question whether the knowledge of His Messianic suffering and death was present to the mind of Jesus from the beginning of His

---

[1] H. L. Strack and P. Billerbeck, *Kommentar zum Neuen Testament aus Talmud und Midrasch*, vols. i–iv.   München, 1922–28.

[2] G. Kittel, *Theologisches Wörterbuch zum Neuen Testament*, vols. i–v. Stuttgart, 1933–.

[3] Especially those of J. Weiss, W. Bousset, R. Bultmann, J. Jeremias, E. Percy, B. W. Bacon, J. Moffatt, C. H. Dodd, T. W. Manson, W. Manson, F. C. Grant, B. S. Easton, J. Knox, and others too numerous to mention.

ministry, or whether this knowledge arose later from the pressure of external events and the development of His thoughts.

In favour of the former view Mk. i. 11, 'Thou art my beloved Son; in thee I am well pleased', and Mk. ii. 20, 'But the days will come when the bridegroom shall be taken away from them', are often quoted; but it may be doubted if they give adequate support. The words of the divine voice at the Baptism of Jesus reflect Psa. ii. 7 and Isa. xlii. 1, and suggest that He is both the Messianic Son and the Servant of God, but there is no allusion to the ideas of Isa. liii, where the Suffering Servant is described. Mk. ii. 20 may well belong to a period after the murder of John the Baptist, especially if the section Mk. ii. i–iii. 6 was compiled before St. Mark's Gospel was written[1] and was taken over much as it stands by the Evangelist. The section is topical and seems to have been compiled in order to show how Jesus came into mortal conflict with the scribes. It seems likely that the older liberals were right when they spoke of 'the Galilean Springtime' in the ministry of Jesus. The knowledge that He would be subjected to a shameful death is certainly present at Caesarea Philippi (Mk. viii. 31) and this expectation may have matured during His retirement to the region of Tyre.[2]

2. A more important question concerns the factors which shaped this expectation. These include the fate of the Old Testament prophets upon which Jesus had manifestly reflected when He said, 'Woe unto you! for you build the tombs of the prophets, and your fathers killed them' (Lk. xi. 47), the death of John the Baptist at the hands of Herod Antipas (Mk. vi. 17–29), the grow-

---

[1] See my commentary, *The Gospel according to St. Mark*, p. 91f.
[2] For a full discussion of this suggestion see my *Life and Ministry of Jesus*.

ing opposition of the scribes and Pharisees (Mk. iii. 6, vii. 1–23, viii. 11–13), the failure, as Jesus interpreted it, of the Galilean Mission, and the influence of Isa. liii. Through reflection, deepened by the experience of communion with God during seasons of prayer, Jesus saw that His suffering and death would be in accord with the will of His Father and were the appointed way to the redemption of sinful men. His lot was to be that of the Suffering and Saving Servant of God. These convictions are expressed in the Passion-sayings of Mk. viii. 31, ix. 12, 31, x. 33f., 45, xiv. 24, and Lk. xvii. 25.

3. A third preliminary question is the authenticity of these sayings. It has often been claimed that they are not authentic utterances of Jesus, but 'community-sayings' which represent the theology of St. Mark and the faith of the primitive church. This question is a crucial issue. Few questions, indeed, in Christian origins are of such importance.

It is probable that among the sayings listed above Mk. x. 33f., with its explicit references to condemnation, the handing over of Jesus to the Gentiles, mocking, spitting, and scourging, is 'a prophecy after the event', for its details correspond closely with the events described in the Passion narratives of St. Mark.[1] The same tendency is to be seen at work in the Matthaean parallel to this saying in which the Evangelist adds a reference to crucifixion (Mt. xx. 19, 'and to crucify'). But I do not think that this explanation can be justly extended to the remaining sayings. Of these Mk. viii. 31, which is expressed in indirect speech, and Mk. ix. 12, 31, and Lk. xvii. 25 may be quoted as examples, leaving Mk. x. 45 and xiv. 24 to be considered later. The sayings mentioned are as follows:

---

[1] Cf. *The Gospel according to St. Mark*, pp. 436–8.

Mk. viii. 31: 'And he began to teach them, that the Son of Man must suffer many things, and be rejected by the elders, and the chief priests, and the scribes, and be killed, and after three days rise again'.
Mk. ix. 12: 'And how is it written of the Son of Man, that he should suffer many things, and be set at nought?'
Mk. ix. 31: 'For he taught his disciples, and said unto them, The Son of Man is delivered into the hands of men, and they will kill him; and when he is killed, after three days he will rise again'.
Lk. xvii. 25: 'But first must he suffer many things and be rejected of this generation.'

In these sayings the details of Mk. x. 33f. are wanting, but there are direct references to suffering, rejection, death, and resurrection. There can be little doubt that the ideas of Isa. liii are presupposed, and this is generally recognized. As we shall see, this debt is even more apparent in Mk. x. 45 and xiv. 24.

In favour of the view that the sayings I have quoted are genuine utterances of Jesus two points may be noted.

(1) It is unsatisfactory to describe these sayings as 'community-sayings'. As B. S. Easton[1] has pointed out, communities may modify sayings in the course of transmission, but the sayings themselves must first exist. They do not arise from the depths of the consciousness of a community, but from the insight of an individual. They reflect prolonged thought on the Servant teaching and are more likely to be His words than those of His followers.

(2) The second consideration is that, while the Servant concept is a characteristic feature of the earliest preaching and teaching, it had become a traditional survival in the period (A.D. 60–70) when St. Mark was written.[2] It appears in the records of the primitive sermons, in Ac. iii.

---

[1] Cf. *The Gospel before the Gospels*, p. 116.
[2] I have developed this argument in detail in an article on 'The Origin of the Markan Passion Sayings' in *New Testament Studies*, vol. I, pp. 159–67.

13, 26, iv. 27, 30. By the time of St. Paul (A.D. 50–60) it is already on the wane, for I Cor. xi. 24, xv. 3f., and Rom. iv. 25, viii. 32, 34 contain ideas which he has taken over from the Jerusalem community, and Phil. ii. 6–11 is being widely recognized as a pre-Pauline hymn. The Servant theology is prominent in I Pet. ii. 22–4, which is not surprising if, as I think, the Epistle is Petrine. In the Pauline Epistles, the Epistle to the Hebrews, and the Johannine writings this theology is overlaid by the Logos Christology. There is a possible allusion to it in Jn. i. 29, 'Behold the Lamb of God who takes away the sin of the world', which, however, is quite general, and may reflect other sacrificial ideas. There is a single example in Heb. ix. 28, 'So also Christ, having been offered once for all to bear the sins of many', and an adaptation of Mk. x. 45 in I Tim. ii. 6, 'Christ Jesus, who gave himself a ransom for all'. Otherwise, it is absent from the Pastoral and Catholic Epistles. Manifestly, in the period A.D. 60–90, when the Gospels were written, the doctrine was in eclipse; it was no longer a living issue. For this reason I find it difficult to think that St. Mark introduced the Servant idea into the Passion-sayings. The presumption is that he records genuine utterances of Jesus.

If this conclusion is accepted it carries us far to the acceptance of Mk. x. 45 and xiv. 24 as genuine words of Jesus. Mk. x. 45, 'For verily the Son of Man came, not to be served, but to serve, and to give his life a ransom for many', has suffered in critical discussions because the metaphor of 'a ransom' has been interpreted in the light of later theories, and especially substitutionary theories of the Atonement. It is not a Pauline metaphor, nor is the language Pauline. The phrase 'for many', which is a recognized Hebraic idiom to express 'for all' is not used by St. Paul and clearly reflects the teaching of Isa. liii. 12.

The same is true of Mk. xiv. 24, 'This is my blood of the covenant, which is shed for many'. Here is added the idea that Christ's death establishes a new covenant between God and men, a covenant which is sealed by His 'blood', that is, by the outpouring of His life in sacrifice. This idea belongs to His teaching.

There is one phrase in the prophecies of the Passion which raises serious difficulties. This is the phrase 'after three days', or as it appears in Matthew and Luke 'the third day'. Can Jesus have spoken so explicitly, since the Resurrection appears to have been unexpected by the disciples? Three things may be said in reply. (1) It is natural that, after speaking of rejection and death, Jesus should speak of resurrection. Isa. liii. 12 speaks of the Servant's exaltation. (2) Preconceived ideas regarding Messiahship made it difficult for the disciples to accept the new teaching. (3) It is possible that the words used by Jesus were less explicit in meaning than they appear to us. In the Old Testament the phrase 'the third day' is sometimes used of a short undefined interval of time. Hos. vi. 2 is an example, 'After two days he will revive us: and on the third day he will raise us up, and we shall live before him'.

I conclude that we are justified in using the Passion-sayings as a clue to the interpretation which Jesus placed upon His suffering and death in spite of the critical problems which these sayings raise. I have felt it necessary to discuss these preliminary questions before we can with a good conscience face the larger issues. They naturally call for a fuller and more detailed treatment than can be given to them in these lectures, but enough, I hope, has been said to show that we are entitled to assume that Jesus had faced the certainty of His death, and had His own interpretation of its meaning.

II. HOW JESUS INTERPRETED HIS CROSS

In considering this question it is difficult to avoid reading back into His sayings the ideas of later times. This possibility must be kept in mind even if the results we reach seem bare. Jesus does not present His teaching in the form of ordered statements after the manner of a philosopher or theologian, and we are dependent upon the sayings which early tradition has preserved. The sayings themselves suggest that His interpretation is likely to have taken the form of prophetic insights shaped by Old Testament ideas and teaching.

1. First, we may say with confidence that He thought of His death in terms of His vocation as the Son of Man. This view is suggested by the form which the Passion-sayings take. Phrases like 'before I suffer' (Lk. xxii. 15) and 'the cup that I shall drink' (Mk. x. 38) are exceptional. Most of the sayings contain the title 'Son of Man'. This means that Jesus interpreted His death in terms of His conception of Messiahship. We have still much to learn about the title and the meaning Jesus found in it. It is clear that He derived it from Dan. vii. 13, which speaks of one 'like unto a son of man' who came to 'the ancient of days' to receive 'dominion, and glory, and a kingdom'. Many scholars have also traced His teaching to the apocalyptic book, I Enoch, in which the Son of Man appears as a super-human figure who is to exercise the functions of judgement in the last days. From the sayings of Jesus it is reasonably clear that He used this name to express His sense of Messiahship in preference to such titles as 'the Son of David' and 'the Christ'.[1] Sometimes, as in Mk. viii. 38 and xiv. 62, it has a futuristic eschatological meaning; it describes Him in

[1] I have discussed these questions in *The Names of Jesus* (1953).

His glory and power at the time of His Parousia or coming. But in other sayings, and in the Passion-sayings in particular, it has a present meaning. The eschatology is 'realised' in the sense that it is expressed here and now in Himself, in spite of the lowliness and humiliation of His earthly lot. One other point must be added. The title is both communal and personal; it describes the Elect Community and the one who is its Head. This idea is perplexing to the western mind, but it is a familiar Old Testament concept, for Hebrew thought closely relates the many and the one, as we see from the use of the pronoun 'I' in the Psalms and in the portraiture of the Servant of the Lord in Isa. liii. Our difficulty is that we cannot sharply distinguish in the Son of Man sayings between the personal and the communal reference. It is clear, however, from the contexts in which many of these sayings appear that the disciples perceived that Jesus was speaking of Himself. When Jesus speaks of the suffering and rejection of the Son of Man, Peter rebukes Him (Mk. viii. 32), and on a later occasion St. Mark explains that Jesus began to tell the disciples the things that were to happen to *Him* (Mk. x. 32). Jesus manifestly believed that suffering, death, and resurrection were involved in the fulfilment of His Messianic ministry.

2. Secondly, Jesus interpreted His vocation as the Son of Man in terms of the idea of the Suffering Servant of the Lord. We are entitled to infer that He had reflected upon the teaching of Isa. liii and had applied it to Himself as the Son of Man. In this Servant poem the unknown prophet of the Exile had said of the Servant, 'Surely he hath borne our griefs, and carried our sorrows. . . . He was wounded for our transgressions, he was bruised for our iniquities: the chastisement of our peace was upon him; and with his stripes we are healed'

(Isa. liii. 4f.). He speaks of him as bearing iniquities (Isa. liii. 11), and he says of him that 'he bare the sin of many, and made intercession for the transgressors' (Isa. liii. 12). At present the question is under debate whether in certain Jewish circles the idea of a Suffering Messiah may not have been pre-Christian. Whether this is so or not, it is Jesus who made the idea current coin and found in it the key to His suffering and death. To what degree He applied to Himself the details of the prophet's portraiture we do not know, for the tradition has not preserved sayings of His which speak of the bearing of sins, that is, of sharing in their burden and consequences, with the exception of Lk. xxii. 37, which quotes Isa. liii. 12, 'And he was reckoned with transgressors'. Yet it can hardly be questioned that He regarded sin-bearing as part of His Messianic destiny, since this is the central conception of Isa. liii, and since He speaks so expressly of giving Himself 'for many' (Mk. x. 45). Moreover, it is in this light that we interpret best His experience in the garden of Gethsemane when He 'began to be greatly amazed and sore troubled', and asked that the 'cup' should be taken away from Him (Mk. xiv. 33, 36). Although not deserted by His Father, it seemed for a while that He was forsaken by Him (Mk. xv. 34).

Unquestionably, it is the role of the Suffering Servant that He believed He was to fulfil. And it is to be noted that this role is more than a personal and individual destiny. It is as the Son of Man that He is to suffer and die, that is, as the Head of the Messianic community. That is why the phrase 'for many' is so characteristic of the Passion-sayings.

3. Lastly, His vocation was interpreted by Jesus in terms of Old Testament conceptions of sacrifice.

This is a difficult conception for the modern man,

repelled as he is by the thought of smoking altars, slain
victims, and streams of blood. He joyfully accepts the
teaching of Mic. vi. 7f., 'Will the Lord be pleased with
thousands of rams, or with ten thousands of rivers of oil?
shall I give my firstborn for my transgression, the fruit
of my body for the sin of my soul?', and with the prophet
he contrasts with these sacrifices doing justly, loving
mercy, and walking humbly with God. But the prophet's
words only reject pagan conceptions of sacrifice and an
unethical reliance upon Old Testament offerings. And
the same is true of still stronger prophetic utterances in
Amos v. 25f., Jer. vii. 21–3, and in Psa. l. 13–15. The
Passion-sayings of Jesus are steeped in sacrificial ideas,
as the references to the idea of a 'ransom' (Mk. x. 45), a
'covenant' and the shedding of blood for many (Mk. xiv.
24), and His use of the Servant concept, attest. He
never speaks of appeasing the anger of God, of placating
Him and causing Him to be gracious to sinners. But
He does use sacrificial ideas as a thought mould. For
Him, we may infer, sacrifice is a representative offering
in which men can share, making it the vehicle or organ
of their own approach to God. In His dying He
expresses the sorrow and penitence which men *ought* to
feel, and which in fellowship with Himself they *do* feel.
He is the Redeemer, the Saviour of the world.

It is in this context of thought that the Lord's Supper,
the Christian Eucharist, is to be understood. During
the last two or three decades more and more attention
has been given by theologians to this rite, which is seen
to stand in the closest connexion with Christ's atoning
work and with His own estimate of its significance. At
the Last Supper, when Jesus said, 'This is my Body'
(Mk. xiv. 22), He meant 'This is I myself', and He
commanded His disciples to take the Bread in this sense

and with this meaning. Their eating was meant to be
an act of self-committal and a sharing in His sacrifice.
Similarly, when He took a cup, and said, 'This is my blood
of the covenant, which is shed for many' (Mk. xiv. 24),
He indicated the act of drinking to be a means of parti-
cipating in His surrendered life offered to God on their
behalf. They were to share in the power of a sacrifice
for which they could claim no merit in themselves.
Substantially the same ideas appear in St. Paul's independent account of the Last Supper in I Cor. xi. 23–5. A
marked feature of the Supper is the close association in it
of sacrificial and eschatological ideas, which stand in no
contradiction, but which not unnaturally received different degrees of emphasis in different primitive communities, as the form of the narratives in Lk. xxii. 14–18
and Mk. xiv. 21–5 suggests. At the Supper Jesus had
the thought of the Kingdom, or Rule, of God in mind
while He spoke of His sacrifice. 'Verily I say unto you',
He said, 'I will no more drink of the fruit of the vine,
until that day when I drink it new in the kingdom of
God' (Mk. xiv. 25). The same thing is said of the bread
in Lk. xxii. 16, and St. Paul says to the Christians of
Corinth, 'For as often as you eat this bread, and drink
the cup, you proclaim the Lord's death until he come'
(I Cor. xi. 26).

The content of the self-offering of Jesus is not indicated
in these sayings, but in the light of what has been already
said we are entitled to think of it in terms of sin-bearing
and as representative. There is more than a suggestion
of a service which He will render at His Parousia in the
words He speaks about His confession before the face of
His Father of those who confess Him before men (Mt.
x. 32, Lk. xii. 8, Mk. viii. 38). So too in the emphasis He
gives to Psa. cx. 1, which includes the words, 'Sit thou on

my right hand' (Mk. xii. 35-7), and which the first Christians quoted so frequently.[1]

III

Such then, so far as we can trace the thought of Jesus in the earliest records, appears to have been the mind of Jesus as He contemplated His Messianic suffering and death. They are the ideas which lie behind the earliest preaching and worship, and they are worked out by the great New Testament teachers, St. Paul, the writer of Hebrews, and St. John. In my submission, these ideas did not originate with the primitive Christian communities or with any of these writers. They are basic original ideas with which Jesus interpreted His Passion. I would stress that they are highly original ideas such as we are entitled to attribute to Jesus Himself. For my part I do not think that we gain a worthy and sufficient doctrine of the Cross, or an adequate standard of Christian living, unless these ideas dominate our religious thinking and worship. They are the foundation motifs of subsequent Christian teaching as we find it reflected in the rest of the New Testament writings. How far this is so, is the question we are to consider as we study what its greatest writers say.

[1] Cf. also the interpretation which J. Jeremias gives to I Cor. xi. 24f. and Lk. xxii. 19b, 'Do this that God may remember me', *The Eucharistic Words of Jesus*, p. 163.

III

THE TEACHING OF ST. PAUL: (I) THE MEANING OF THE CROSS

Archbishop Temple has observed that there are those who pay visits to St. John as to a fascinating foreign country, but come home to St. Paul, and that there are others who find St. Paul the exciting and also rather bewildering adventure, but with St. John are at home. Bishop Charles Gore, he said, belonged to the former group, but he himself to the latter; with St. John he was 'at home'. This distinction is very true of biblical students. In this lecture I trust I may be able to show that, if the study of St. Paul is the exciting and rather bewildering adventure, the journey is well worth while.

I. PAUL'S DEBT TO PRIMITIVE CHRISTIANITY

A marked trend in modern biblical study is the recognition that primitive Christian teaching, on which all the New Testament writers depend, was much richer and fuller than we had supposed. St. Paul leans heavily upon this teaching. He himself refers to it in I Cor. xv. 3f.: 'For I delivered unto you first of all that which also I received, how that Christ died for our sins according to the scriptures; and that he was buried; and that he hath been raised on the third day according to the scriptures . . .'. The words 'delivered' and 'received' are terms normally used of the imparting and receiving of tradition, and 'first of all' means 'first in importance'.

24

Much that was formerly described as 'Pauline' is primitive teaching taken over, interpreted, and expanded.

Among the primitive ideas connected with the Cross which St. Paul adopts are the necessity of Christ's death in the purpose of God; its Messianic character; its vicarious, representative, and sacrificial aspects; its connexion with sin, with faith, and sacramental communion; its fruits in the moral and spiritual life. Even his emphasis upon the universality of its benefits only develops what was already implicit in primitive belief, in spite of hesitation regarding table-fellowship with Gentiles. To these ideas St. Paul gives a deeper impress. Other ideas, we shall see, are more characteristic of his teaching.

No one can fail to observe the deep feeling with which he writes. He speaks of the Galatians as his little children, of whom he is again in travail until Christ be formed in them. 'I could wish to be present with you now', he writes, 'and to change my voice; for I am perplexed about you' (Gal. iv. 20). To the Corinthians he writes, 'Who is weak, and I am not weak? who is made to stumble, and I burn not?' (2 Cor. xi. 29). 'Even unto this present hour', he says, 'we both hunger, and thirst, and are naked, and are buffeted, and have no certain dwellingplace; and we toil, working with our own hands: being reviled, we bless; being persecuted, we endure; being defamed, we entreat: we are made as the filth of the world, the offscouring of all things, even until now' (I Cor. iv. 11–13).

This same emotion is present in all that he says of the Cross. St. Paul is not a formal theologian, but a poet and a rhapsodist. Yet beneath all his deep feeling there is a keen and scintillating mind, which challenges his readers by the daring of his epigrams and the greatness of his thought.

c

It is natural that his vocabulary should contain new words and phrases. Forgiveness is sparingly mentioned. St. Paul prefers to speak of Justification and Reconciliation. He alone uses the phrase 'the death of Christ' or 'His death', and, apart from 'the Cross' in Heb. xii. 2, he is the only New Testament writer to speak of 'the Cross of Christ'. He also uses such phrases as 'living', 'dying', and 'rising with Christ', and speaks frequently of being 'in Christ' or 'in Him'. His teaching reveals that he thinks of Christ's death as both a saving event and as the focal point of a rich Christian experience. In the present lecture the former will be considered. The latter will be treated in the lecture which follows.

A word must be added on the interpretation of St. Paul's teaching. It is useless to impose a fictitious unity upon it. St. Paul is one of those writers who are prepared to risk being misunderstood. While he has dominating ideas, he will sometimes introduce aspects not otherwise articulated with the rest of his teaching. Again, he interprets the Old Testament freely, not always concerning himself with its original meaning as a modern student would. Further, on occasion his arguments are rabbinical, as, for example, when he contrasts the freewoman Sarah with the handmaid Hagar, and says of the story, 'Which things are an allegory'. So also he makes much of the word 'seed' in the passage about Abraham in Gal. iii. 16, and comments, 'He says not, And to seeds, as of many; but as of one, And to thy seed, which is Christ'. Or again, after referring to the rock, which according to current exegesis followed the Israelites in the wilderness, he quietly adds, 'And the rock was Christ' (I Cor. x. 4). St. Paul must be read with sympathy and with intelligence.

Many analogies are used which must not be pressed too far. Some of these are legal, as when he says, 'God condemned sin in the flesh' (Rom. viii. 3); some have to do with the manumission of slaves, as in the words, 'You were bought with a price' (I Cor. vi. 20); and some are commercial, as in the passage, 'And it was reckoned to him for righteousness' (Rom. iv. 3). These analogies must not be turned into precise scientific statements. This warning applies especially to his most daring flights, as when he says that Christ was 'made to be sin on our behalf' (2 Cor. v. 21) and became 'a curse for us' (Gal. iii. 13).

In the next section I propose to indicate the manner in which St. Paul describes Christ's saving deed. To separate his teaching upon this matter from all that he writes of faith, justification, and reconciliation is dangerous and misleading, unless we see what we are doing. Nevertheless, in the interests of exposition this separation is necessary. No harm is done if we remember that this is but part of his teaching.

II. ST. PAUL'S ACCOUNT OF CHRIST'S SAVING DEED

1. *First, its cosmic aspects must be noted.* This is an aspect of Christ's saving work which is strange to the modern man. St. Paul could not ignore it because of the existence of ancient beliefs current in his day, in which he himself, as a man of his time, shared. It is mentioned from time to time in his letters, but it is not woven closely into the texture of his thinking, and is not of permanent value except in one important respect to be mentioned later.

Throughout the world of St. Paul's day it was believed that the universe, especially the upper air and the stars, was peopled by spiritual powers or beings hostile to man. This belief is the key to St. Paul's words when he writes,

'Our wrestling is not against flesh and blood, but against the principalities, against the powers, against the world-rulers of this darkness, against the spiritual hosts of wickedness in the heavenly places' (Eph. vi. 12). It also explains why, when he speaks of the things that cannot separate us from the love of God in Christ, he mentions, not only life or death, and things present or things to come, but also angels, principalities, and powers (Rom. viii. 38f.). He speaks also of 'the rulers of this world' (I Cor. ii. 6, 8) and of 'elemental spirits'[1] (Gal. iv. 9 and Col. ii. 8).

It was natural, therefore, that he should speak of the saving deed of Christ against this background of thought. That is why he attributes the crucifixion of Christ to 'the rulers of this world', by which he does not mean kings and governors. These rulers did not know God's wisdom, he declares, 'for had they known it, they would not have crucified the Lord of glory' (I Cor. ii. 8). The most striking example of this strand in his teaching is Col. ii. 15, in which he speaks of the triumph of Christ. 'Having put off from himself the principalities and the powers', he writes, 'he made a show of them openly, triumphing over them in it', that is, in the Cross.

Here, doubtless, is a mode of thought in respect of which Bultmann's plea,[2] that we need to demythologize the New Testament, has force, but if we attempt to do this, his warning must be remembered that we must interpret the mythology, and not merely eliminate it. If this is done, it is evident that St. Paul's teaching means that Christ's victory over evil is complete. There are no pockets of resistance left, and its present ravages are those

[1] Not 'rudiments'.
[2] See his essay, 'New Testament and Mythology', reprinted in *Kerygma and Myth* (edited by H. W. Bartsch).

of a beaten foe. God's purpose, as St. Paul sees it, is to
reconcile all things through Christ to Himself, 'whether
things upon the earth, or things in the heavens' (Col. i.
20). Who can fail to see the grandeur of his thought?

2. *Secondly, and more important, St. Paul closely relates
Christ's saving deed to the fact of sin.* He strongly underlines and expands the primitive confession, 'Christ died
for our sins' (I Cor. xv. 3). Thus, he speaks of 'Our
Lord Jesus Christ, who gave himself for our sins' (Gal. i.
4), 'who was delivered up for our trespasses, and raised
for our justification' (Rom. iv. 25). By 'sin' he under-
stands, not only sinful acts, such as theft, lying, and
murder, but also a *state* in which man finds himself, and
which is expressed in self-assertion, self-coronation, and
rebellion against God. One is reminded of that scene in
Shakespeare's *Second Part of King Henry IV*, in which
Prince Henry comes to the bedside of his sleeping father
and puts the crown upon his own head.

> 'Lo, here it sits—
Which God shall guard: and put the world's whole strength
Into one giant arm, it shall not force
This lineal honour from me: this from thee
Will I to mine leave, as 'tis left to me.'

Sometimes St. Paul almost personifies sin, as when he
says, 'Let not sin therefore reign in your mortal body'
(Rom. vi. 12), and declares, 'Sin shall not have dominion
over you' (Rom. vi. 14), and again when he says of 'the
bond written in ordinances that was against us' that
Christ has blotted it out, and has taken it out of the way
'nailing it to the cross' (Col. ii. 14). In Christ, he exults,
'we have our redemption through his blood, the forgiveness of our trespasses' (Eph. i. 7). Sin is an alien power,
from which we are delivered through Christ's 'blood',
that is, by His life freely surrendered in death.

3. *Thirdly, St. Paul speaks of this saving deed in various ways.* (*a*) *Its source is God's love.* 'God commends his own love, in that, while we were yet sinners, Christ died for us' (Rom. v. 8). This statement shows that any interpretation of the Cross which implies that the death of the Son changes the attitude of the Father towards men, is un-Pauline. The same emphasis is seen in another of St. Paul's greatest utterances, 'In Christ God was reconciling the world to himself' (2 Cor. v. 19). (*b*) *It is a deed wrought for the undeserving.* It is an unswerving Pauline conviction that man can have no claim before God. He cannot win or deserve his salvation. He can only receive it as a gift in humble dependence upon God. St. Paul is fully conscious of the amazing character of this Gospel. He precedes the passage quoted above about God's love by the well known words, 'For scarcely for a righteous man will one die: for peradventure for the good man some one would even dare to die' (Rom. v. 7). It is the distinguishing of God's work in Christ that it is for sinners. This is the truth pictured by Christ in the Parable of the Prodigal Son, although here, of course, there is no allusion to the doctrine of the Atonement. (*c*) *Further, this deed is wrought on their behalf.* This is the sense in which he consistently uses the preposition 'for'. He never uses the Greek preposition which means 'instead of'. And he avoids—one must say deliberately—the words which mean 'ransom', 'redeemer', and 'to redeem'.[1] He does use the word 'redemption', which belongs to this family of words, but in the sense of deliverance from sin or from judgement, not from punishment. He even avoids the word 'mediator' when speaking of Christ's work, although he uses the term of Moses and the giving of the law (Gal. iii. 19f.). This usage means that St.

---

[1] The Greek *lutron* and its cognates.

Paul's doctrine is not substitutionary. He does not teach that Christ suffered or was punished in our stead. He grazes the edge of substitution when he says that 'one died for all' and that 'therefore all died' (2 Cor. v. 14), and again when he says that Christ was 'made to be sin on our behalf' (2 Cor. v. 21) and that He became 'a curse for us' (Gal. iii. 13). But even in these passages his word is 'on our behalf', not 'in our stead'. Of course, in St. Paul's teaching Christ's death is substitutionary in the sense that He did for us that which we can never do for ourselves, but not in the sense that He transfers our punishment to Himself, so that we have nothing to do but to accept His benefits. St. Paul seems to have shared the unwillingness of the modern man to think in this way. But the deeper reason is that he sees a dynamic quality in Christ's saving deed, which is wrought *in us* as well as *for us*, and in which in our own measure we are permitted to share. This truth will become clearer when we go on to consider his teaching concerning the Cross in Christian experience.

4. *Fourthly, then, so far as we can characterize St. Paul's view of Christ's saving deed, we must say that it is the act of a representative.* This appears from those passages, so strange to the reader of today, in which he speaks of Christ as 'the Second Adam' (Rom. v. 12–21, I Cor. xv. 45). In these passages St. Paul thinks of Christ as the Head of a new order in humanity corresponding to the place occupied by Adam in contemporary Jewish teach- ing. It is somewhat surprising that he does not explicitly speak of sin-bearing, perhaps because he makes so little use of the idea of the Suffering Servant. But in the epigram 'made to be sin on our behalf' he implies that Christ experienced the gloom and penalty of human sin by submitting in love to the judgement of God which

rests upon it. John Woolman in his Diary wrote, 'I felt the depth and the extent of the misery of my fellow-creatures, separated from the Divine Harmony, and it was more than I could bear'. Probably St. Paul attributed a suffering of this kind to Christ. 'The wages of sin', he wrote, 'is death' (Rom. vi. 23), and, while he expressly describes Christ as 'Him who knew no sin', he must have been thinking of His subjection to its penalty when he continued, 'He (that is, God) made (him) to be sin on our behalf' (2 Cor. v. 21). This problem we shall have to consider later. Here we can only note St. Paul's view that, in virtue of His relationship to man, as the Second Adam, Christ suffered with the guilty.

St. Paul does not discuss this problem in detail, as theologians in later times have been compelled to do. Neither does he present us with a theory of Christ's atoning deed. His nearest approach to such an explanation is Rom. iii. 25f., in which he describes Christ's work in its dual relationship to God and man in terms of Justification. He speaks of 'being justified freely by his grace through the redemption that is in Christ Jesus', and then writes:

'Whom God set forth to be a propitiation, through faith, by his blood, to shew his righteousness, because of the passing over of the sins done aforetime, in the forbearance of God; for the shewing, I say, of his righteousness at this present season: that he might himself be just, and the justifier of him that hath faith in Jesus.'

This passage deserves the closest study. 'A propitiation' is a misleading rendering of the adjective *hilasterion* which St. Paul uses of Christ, for he does not speak of Christ's deed as one of appeasement, and the translation is contrary to the dominant usage of the Greek Bible.[1] Many commentators prefer the attractive rendering 'Mercy Seat', but I doubt if this is St. Paul's idea. The

[1] See C. H. Dodd, *The Bible and the Greeks*, pp. 82–95.

best interpretation seems to me that God set forth Christ 'as a means of expiation' or 'atonement', that is, 'as one covering sins'. 'By his blood' means 'by his life freely surrendered in death', and 'by faith' suggests that what Christ has done for us is to be apprehended, and made our own, through complete dependence upon Him. 'The righteousness of God' is His saving activity, which might appear to have been compromised by His forbearance, but is now made known. The words 'just' and 'justifier' describe God, who, in consequence of Christ's saving deed, is seen to be righteous and is revealed as the One who gives a righteous standing to the man who believes in Christ. There is nothing small in this passage. It describes the nature and results of Christ's deed upon the grandest scale.

5. *Lastly, St. Paul uses, although with a certain reserve, the language of sacrifice to describe the saving ministry of Christ.* His use of the term 'blood' in the passage quoted above, and in other passages, shows this. It is a suggestive usage, not lightly to be lost, for if instead of 'by his blood' we use some such phrase as 'through Christ crucified', the primary suggestion is that of an event rather than its significance as the offering of dedicated life. St. Paul is endorsing traditional ideas when he records the saying concerning the eucharistic cup in the form, 'This cup is the new covenant in my blood' (I Cor. xi. 25); but he makes use of sacrificial ideas himself when he writes, 'For our passover has been sacrificed, even Christ' (I Cor. v. 7), and still more when he says, 'Walk in love, even as Christ also loved you, and gave himself up for us, an offering and a sacrifice to God for an odour of a sweet smell' (Eph. v. 2). It cannot be said, however, that he makes a pronounced use of sacrificial ideas, certainly not to the extent to which they appear in the Epistle to the Hebrews, and proportionately

not to the degree to which they underlie the Passion-sayings in Mark. Upon this matter conjectures alone are possible, but they remain conjectures, and the isolated reference which he makes to Christ's intercession on high in Rom. viii. 34, in the words, 'Who is at the right hand of God, who also makes intercession for us', warns us against exaggeration. He has no hesitation in speaking of his own sufferings in sacrificial language, as in Phil. ii. 17, where he says, 'Yea, and if I am poured out as a drink-offering upon the sacrifice and service of your faith, I joy, and rejoice with you all' (cf. 2 Tim. iv. 6), and in Rom. xv. 16 he speaks of himself as 'ministering (mg. 'ministering in sacrifice') the gospel of God, that the offering up of the Gentiles might be made acceptable, being sanctified by the Holy Spirit'. It is not fanciful to trace this language to St. Paul's apprehension of the meaning of the Cross. We are entitled to say that, while sacrificial ideas do not supply the main category in which he sets forth the idea of Christ's representative ministry, they do enter into his teaching and colour his thought.

III. THE VALUE OF ST. PAUL'S TEACHING

The brief account I have given of St. Paul's estimate of Christ's saving deed reveals his dependence upon primitive Christian teaching and, it is hoped, the manner in which he developed and expanded it. Christian theology owes an immeasurable debt to the Apostle to the Gentiles. His immediate influence upon later writers does not compare with that exerted by him in the subsequent centuries, especially upon Augustine and at the Reformation, and down to the present day. Even more is this true of his teaching concerning the Cross in relation to the Christian experience. To this question we shall turn in the next lecture.

IV

THE TEACHING OF ST. PAUL: (II) THE CROSS IN CHRISTIAN EXPERIENCE

I N this lecture I propose to discuss the manner in which St. Paul connects the saving deed of Christ with the experience of the believer. I have already spoken of the danger of separating the two themes by the assumption that his doctrine of the Cross is complete in itself, so that the Christian experience is only a deduction from it. According to St. Paul's teaching, one cannot apprehend the meaning of the Cross apart from the experience, nor the experience apart from the Cross. Bultmann's discussion, in his essay 'New Testament and Mythology', illustrates this danger. Here everything is staked on the experience; the doctrine is described as mythological, although at the same time it is recognized that the event of Jesus is the revelation of the love of God. 'To believe in the cross of Christ', Bultmann says, 'does not mean to concern ourselves with a mythical process wrought outside of us and our world, or with an objective event turned by God to our advantage, but rather to make the cross of Christ our own, to undergo crucifixion with him.'[1] This statement is impressive, but one is bound to ask how it is possible to speak of being crucified with Christ without a fuller knowledge of what crucifixion meant for Him. Will not also crucifixion with Christ at least reflect, and so help us to understand, what the Cross means? The persuasion that there is an intimate

[1] *Kerygma and Myth*, p. 36.

35

connexion between the deed and the experience is the
view which this lecture seeks to unfold.

I. THE CHRISTIAN EXPERIENCE IN RELATION TO THE SAVING DEED OF CHRIST

The themes which call for discussion are Faith in
Christ, Faith Union with Him, Sacramental Communion,
and Sacrificial Living.[1]

1. *Faith in Christ.* St. Paul uses the noun 'faith' and
the verb 'to believe' in the sense of trusting. Sometimes
confidence in God's word or promise is meant. This
confidence is illustrated in the account he gives of
Abraham's faith when, quoting Gen. xv. 6, he says,
'And Abraham believed God, and it was reckoned to
him for righteousness' (Rom. iv. 3). Strong emphasis is
laid upon his trust in God's promise of a son. 'Without
being weakened in faith he considered his own body
now as good as dead'. 'He wavered not through unbelief,
but waxed strong through faith, giving glory to God,
and being fully assured that, what he had promised, he
was able also to perform' (Rom. iv. 20f.). Again, St.
Paul stresses the importance of faith when speaking of
'the Gospel'. 'It is the power of God unto salvation', he
says, 'to every one that believes. . . . For therein is
revealed a righteousness of God by faith unto faith: as it
is written, But the righteous shall live by faith' (Rom.
i. 16f.).

Especially characteristic of St. Paul's teaching is his
view of faith as dependence, utter and complete, upon
Christ. We are justified 'by faith' (Rom. v. 1, Gal. ii. 16,
iii. 24). It is by grace that we have been saved 'through

---

[1] I have fully discussed the Pauline themes of Forgiveness, Justification,
Reconciliation, Fellowship, and Sanctification in *Forgiveness and Reconciliation.*

faith' (Eph. ii. 8), and it is 'through faith' that Christ
dwells in our hearts (Eph. iii. 17). Life itself for St. Paul
is rooted in Christ who died. 'That life which I now
live in the flesh', he declares, 'I live in faith, the faith
which is in the Son of God, who loved me, and gave
himself up for me' (Gal. ii. 20). Here is an unmistakable
link between faith as a way of life and Christ's death,
and it is one which cannot be ignored without mis-
understanding St. Paul's theology. Faith is the under-
tone to all that he says concerning the Christian experience.

It is not surprising that, whenever the greatness of St.
Paul's teaching has been recovered, as, for example, by
Augustine, Luther, and Wesley, this master key of his
theology has been grasped. An example is provided by
Wesley's well known account of his visit to a religious
society in Aldersgate Street, London, when one was
reading Luther's Preface to the Epistle to the Romans.
'About a quarter before nine', he writes, 'while he was
describing the change which God works in the heart
through faith in Christ, I felt my heart strangely warmed.
I felt I did trust in Christ, Christ alone, for salvation;
and an assurance was given me that He had taken away
my sins, even *mine*, and saved *me* from the law of sin and
death'. This discovery is reflected in Wesley's definition
of faith in Christ, as 'a recumbency upon Him as our atonement and our life, as given for us, and living in us: and,
in consequence hereof, a closing with Him, and cleaving to
Him . . .'. In these words the connexion between faith
and Christ's work is clearly evident, and the definition is
fully Pauline.

In particular, this connexion appears in St. Paul's
teaching concerning Justification and Reconciliation. By
reason of its derivation Justification has a legal ring, but
in St. Paul's usage its meaning is warm and personal. It

is the act of God in putting men right with Himself. In *Forgiveness and Reconciliation*[1] I have pointed out that St. Paul derived his vocabulary from Jewish teaching concerning the Last Judgement, and that the significant thing in his usage is that he transfers the idea of acquittal to the present. Here and now, he maintains, when there is no claim to merit or desert, God declares righteous the man whose faith is in Jesus. Christ's death, he teaches, is the ground or basis of Justification. We are 'justified by his blood' (Rom. v. 9). We are 'justified freely by his grace through the redemption that is in Christ Jesus' (Rom. iii. 24). There is no 'moral fiction' in this act of God, any more than there is in the Parable of the Prodigal Son, where, while the son was afar off, 'his father saw him, and was moved with compassion, and ran, and fell on his neck, and kissed him' (Lk. xv. 20). The genuine exercise of faith is one of the purest moments in a man's life, when, crying 'I have sinned', he claims nothing for himself, but casts himself utterly upon God, like the tax-gatherer in the Parable of Lk. xviii. 9–14 of whom Jesus said, 'This man went down to his house justified rather than the other', that is, the Pharisee who thanked God that he was not as the rest of men. Justifying faith derives its moral content from the Christ in whom it rests and who freely gave Himself for the redemption of men. In the moment of its exercise the sinner is righteous, not as yet in moral attainment, but in spirit and in promise. In the realm of fiction Jean Valgean, in the story of the bishop's candlesticks in *Les Misérables* is an example, and other parallels meet us in daily life.

I remember during World War I seeing a group of raw recruits undergoing training as cavalrymen. Were they soldiers? The sergeant seemed doubtful. He

---

[1] *Op. cit.*, pp. 48–53.

insinuated that they were not sure which was the head
and which the tail of their horses. Their uniforms did
not fit, but they were certainly soldiers. They had cast
the die, they had taken the oath, and later they were to
prove their worth upon the fields of Flanders.

Like many illustrations this is an imperfect analogy,
but it meets the objection in question. The righteousness
of the justified man is immature, but it is real, and therefore can be recognized as such. It is not of any man's
achieving, but is born in the act of faith. Its efficacy is
derived from the power of Christ's saving deed. That is
why the Apostle speaks of 'being justified by his blood'
(Rom. v. 9). God puts the believing man right with
Himself because, through faith in the Crucified, he has
righteous desires and a righteous will.

Reconciliation has the same implications. By it St.
Paul means the act of God in restoring men to fellowship
with Himself. It is the mending of broken relationships,
a restoration effected by Him. The process of growth
arising out of it is Sanctification, a daily growing in
perfect love which is co-extensive with life and is consummated in eternity. 'I count not myself yet to have apprehended', writes St. Paul, 'but one thing I do, forgetting
the things which are behind, and stretching forward to
the things which are before, I press on toward the goal of
the high calling of God in Christ Jesus' (Phil. iii. 13f.).

The immediate and decisive character of Reconciliation
is implied when St. Paul says that 'we also rejoice in God
through our Lord Jesus Christ, through whom we have
now received the reconciliation' (Rom. v. 11). It is a
state of peace with God made possible because we are
justified by faith (Rom. v. 1f.). And equally with Justification St. Paul connects Reconcilation with the death of
Christ. He is so sure of this connexion that he can make

it an assumption, a condition leading to a further claim. 'If, while we were enemies, we were reconciled to God', he argues, 'through the death of his Son, much more, being reconciled, shall we be saved by his life' (Rom. v. 10). In Eph. ii. 16 the reconciliation of Jew and Gentile 'in one body unto God' is 'through the cross'. In this teaching St. Paul is speaking of the Christian experience, and again the experience throws light upon the saving deed from which it springs. The Cross was such a dealing with sin as to make Reconciliation possible. St. Paul himself does not work out this thought, but theology is fully justified in doing so in terms of Pauline thought. Sin is not, and was not, dismissed with the wave of an indulgent hand by God; it was recognized, borne, and confessed by Christ. All this is implied by the declaration that, in Christ, God was reconciling the world to Himself (2 Cor. v. 19).

Enough perhaps has been said to reveal the rich content which St. Paul finds in Faith in Christ and its connexion with His death. But the Apostle has a richer conception to unfold when he speaks of Faith Union with Christ.

2. *Faith Union with Christ.* This union is not something fundamentally different from faith, but faith itself in the closeness of personal communion with Christ. It is not a 'mystical' relationship involving the loss of personal identity, as when the drop mingles with the ocean, but a fellowship of love in which thoughts, desires, and intentions are mutually shared. This union with Christ is often expressed by the phrases 'in Christ', 'in the Lord', and 'in Him'. A. Deissmann counted 164 examples in the major epistles of St. Paul, but not all of them have to do with the idea of faith-union. In many cases 'by Christ' or 'by Him' would be an adequate translation. The faith relationship is expressed when St.

Paul bids his readers reckon themselves 'alive unto God in Christ Jesus' (Rom. vi. 11), when he describes 'the mystery among the Gentiles' as 'Christ in you, the hope of glory' (Col. i. 27), and in such counsels as 'Walk in him, rooted and builded up in him' (Col. ii. 7). Alternatively in Gal. ii. 20 St. Paul speaks of Christ living in him. The idea of union with Christ is brought into connexion with His death when he writes, 'Now in Christ Jesus you that were once afar off are made nigh in the blood of Christ' (Eph. ii. 13).

More vivid and picturesque are the passages in which St. Paul speaks of suffering, dying, rising, and living with Christ. Limited to the Pauline and the Pastoral Epistles, these phrases describe a spiritual experience, arising out of the faith relationship, in which the believer participates in the Passion and Resurrection of Christ. St. Paul says of himself, 'I have been crucified with Christ' (Gal. ii. 20), and to the Christians at Rome he writes, 'If we died with Christ, we believe that we shall also live with him' (Rom. vi. 8). His prayer is that he may gain Christ and be found 'in him', that he may know him, 'and the power of his resurrection, and the fellowship of his sufferings, becoming conformed to his death' (Phil. iii. 9f.). This language expresses in the Pauline idiom ideas parallel to those of Jesus, when He spoke of drinking His cup (Mk. x. 39) and of cross-bearing (Mk. viii. 34), and when He took with Him Peter, James, and John into the garden of Gethsemane, and said to them, 'Pray that you enter not into temptation' (Lk. xxii. 40).

The presence of the same kind of teaching in St. Paul's treatment of Baptism, as baptism into Christ's death, I shall consider in the next section. Meantime the relation of this teaching to Christ's saving ministry claims attention.

D

In speaking of suffering and dying with Christ St. Paul has no thought of suggesting that Christ's work is incomplete. Quite the reverse is true. Nevertheless, he refuses to isolate the Christian experience from the Cross. Thus, he can speak of the sufferings incurred in his own missionary labours as filling up that which remains over of the afflictions of Christ (Col. i. 24). In these afflictions he himself shares, and from his teaching as a whole we must infer his belief that a participation of this kind is the privilege of Christians in general. Pascal has observed that 'It is one of the great principles of Christianity, that all that happened to Jesus Christ must fulfil itself in the spirit and body of every Christian'. And, on reflection, few Christians with any depth of understanding can doubt the truth of this claim. This suffering with Christ must involve some knowledge of the bearing of sins. The shame of moral degradation visible in individuals and communities is felt most by those least guilty of it. Complacency in this matter, like that of Jonah who went out from Nineveh, and sat in the shadow under his tent, 'till he might see what would become of the city' (Jon. iv. 5), is not possible. No less true is this of the love of God revealed in the Cross. The Christian must reflect it too. I remember a man known to me many years ago whose face shone with this love. Men turned round to look at him in the street. As in the case of Stephen, 'God's glory smote him on the face'. Few of us, let us hope, have failed to meet with examples of dying and living with Christ.

3. *Sacramental Communion with Christ.* Let it be said at once that this kind of communion with Christ does not differ fundamentally from those already described. It is a faith relationship with Christ which is necessarily communal in its expression since it is experienced in con-

nexion with rites which from the beginning the first communities connected with the saving deed of Christ, and which they believed to be of His appointing. These rites are Baptism into the name of Christ and the Lord's Supper. As St. Paul describes them they are not magical in their operation, but spiritual, provided that we remember that by 'spiritual' St. Paul includes the whole nature of man, body and soul, and not a part of his being in the Greek sense of the term. I do not myself believe that it is necessary to explain St. Paul's sacramental teaching as the product of Hellenistic influences connected with the 'mystery-religions'; they are basically Jewish in origin shaped by the remembrance of Christ's words and actions. This view applies to Baptism as well as to the Lord's Supper, for to separate the two in thinking of St. Paul's teaching is mistaken.

St. Paul's distinctive teaching concerning Baptism is found in Rom. vi. 3–6. It is significant that it is developed in connexion with the ideas of dying and living with Christ (Rom. vi. 2). 'Are you ignorant', he asks his readers, 'that all we who were baptized into Christ Jesus were baptized into his death?' (Rom. vi. 3). The act of immersion reminds him of the imagery of burial and death followed by resurrection, and he continues, 'We were buried therefore with him through baptism into death: that like as Christ was raised from the dead through the glory of the Father, so we also might walk in newness of life' (Rom. vi. 4). It will be seen that St. Paul thinks of Baptism as an expression in action of that faith union with Christ of which he speaks repeatedly. This view emerges clearly in the comment which follows, if in terms of his teaching we interpret expressions which otherwise are strange to the modern reader.

'For if we have become united with him by the likeness of his
death, we shall be also by the likeness of his resurrection; knowing
this, that our old man was crucified with him, that the body of
sin might be done away, that so we should no longer be in bondage
to sin' (Rom. vi. 5f.).

The phrase 'our old man' means in modern language 'the
old self' unrenewed by Christ, and the expression 'the
body of sin' is 'the sinful self' which otherwise is dominant in man. This meaning becomes clear if we observe
that in St. Paul's psychological vocabulary 'the body' is
not always what he calls the 'mortal body' (Rom. vi. 12,
viii. 11), but 'the person' or 'self', as in Rom. xii. 1 and
in other passages.[1] We shall understand his meaning
better in some such rendering as this, 'Our old self
was crucified with him, that the sinful self might be
abolished, that so we should no longer be slaves to
sin'.

If we consider this teaching we shall see that St. Paul
does not attach any mystic significance to water, and we
know from I Cor. i. 14–17 that he was far from magnify-
ing the importance of rites as such. But he does believe
that, where there is moral and spiritual union with Christ,
Baptism, like prophetic action in the Old Testament,
effects that which it symbolizes.[2]

St. Paul's teaching concerning the Lord's Supper
develops similar ideas. He takes over the words of Jesus
from tradition[3] in a form which adds to the saying, 'This
is my body', the phrase 'which is for you', and gives the

---

[1] For a fuller discussion see my commentary on the *Epistle to the Romans*,
(1955) p. 15 in the Epworth Preacher's Commentaries Series.

[2] For examples of prophetic symbolism in the Old Testament see Isa.
viii. 3, xx. 2, Jer. xix. 10, xxviii. 10, Ezek. iv. 3, Ac. xxi. 11. I have
treated this question in *Jesus and His Sacrifice*, p. 118f.

[3] That the tradition Paul attests is later than that embodied in Mk. xiv.
22, 24 is maintained in my commentary on Mark, p. 546.

saying regarding the wine in the words, 'This cup is the new covenant in my blood' ; and in each case he has the command, 'Do this in remembrance of me' (I Cor. xi. 23–5). A connexion with Christ's saving deed is established in his comment, 'For as often as you eat this bread, and drink the cup, you proclaim the Lord's death till he come' (I Cor. xi. 26). His further warnings against eating or drinking 'unworthily' and failing to discern the body show that he thinks of the rite as more than a symbolic memorial meal, and this inference is raised to a certainty by I Cor. x. 16, in which he asks, 'The cup of blessing which we bless, is it not a communion of the blood of Christ? The bread which we break, is it not a communion of the body of Christ?' If, as we have seen, the 'blood' is the life of Christ poured out in sacrifice, and the 'body' is Christ's self, St. Paul's considered view is that the Lord's Supper is the opportunity to participate, or share, in the blessings and in the power of His death. There is thus a 'Catholic', as well as a 'Protestant', strain in his teaching, although he has nothing to say about 'transubstantiation' or the offering of Christ as Victim upon the altar. His teaching is well expressed by Charles Wesley in the lines:

'This eucharistic feast
Our every want supplies;
And still we by His death are blessed,
And share His sacrifice.'

4. *Sacrificial Living.* St. Paul's teaching upon this theme is intimately related to all that he writes about the faith relationship with Christ. The fact that usually in his Epistles he treats doctrinal issues first and then writes his hortatory sections, as in Romans, Galatians, and Colossians, tends to obscure this vital connexion; but the content of his exhortations makes it perfectly

clear. The Christian life, as he describes it, is the out-flowing of faith in the Crucified.

In order to illustrate this connexion fully it would be necessary to dwell upon the greater part of his ethical teaching. To do this in the present lecture is not possible, but, fortunately, some of his most characteristic utterances make the relationship immediately clear. Thus, in Rom. xii. 1 he writes in well known words, 'I beseech you therefore, brethren, by the mercies of God, to present your bodies a living sacrifice, holy, acceptable to God, which is your reasonable (mg. 'spiritual') service'. This is one of the passages in which 'selves' represents St. Paul's thought better than 'bodies'. Again, when urging the strong to bear the infirmities of the weak, he recalls the fact that 'Christ also pleased not himself' (Rom. xv. 3), and he applies to Him the words of Psa. lxix. 9, 'The reproaches of them that reproached thee fell upon me'. Further, when urging his readers to be 'kind one to another, tenderhearted, forgiving each other', he adds, 'even as God also in Christ forgave you' (Eph. iv. 32). There are no doctrinal allusions of this kind in the 'Hymn to Love' in I Cor. xiii, but there can be no doubt that the love of which he writes is a love he has found embodied in the Cross.

Perhaps the most striking illustration of this connexion between the Christian life and the Cross is to be seen in the 'Hymn to Christ' in Phil. ii. 6–11. At present there is a tendency among many New Testament scholars to explain the passage as a pre-Pauline hymn on grounds of vocabulary and style. The arguments are not conclusive, but in any case St. Paul has used the hymn to express his deepest convictions about Christ's person and work. Everything in it gives point to his exhortation, 'Have this mind in you which was also in Christ Jesus' (Phil.

ii. 5), precisely as he appeals to 'the grace of our Lord Jesus Christ' in 2 Cor. viii. 9. This 'mind', he shows, was manifest in Christ's renunciation of the Divine Glory, who, although originally in the form of God, did not think of equality with God as a thing to be clutched, but emptied himself. It was manifest also in His acceptance of a complete humanity, when, taking the form of a slave, He was made in the likeness of men, and, in particular, in the humiliation of His Cross. With a force which must have made a deep impression on his Philippian readers, who prided themselves on their Roman citizenship, he says, 'He humbled himself, becoming obedient even unto death, yes, the death of a cross'. Finally, it was manifest in His exaltation, which revealed that Christ is Lord even in the time of that humiliation, so that He is given by God the name that is above every name, 'that in the name of Jesus every knee should bow, in heaven, and on earth, and under the earth, and that every tongue should confess that Jesus Christ is Lord, to the glory of God the Father'. It is this 'mind' that we are to have. If questioned, St. Paul would have said that we can neither earn it, nor buy it, nor copy it. We can only receive it from Him who died for us and lives in us. In the words of Heinrich Müller,

> 'Thus, at His love, my love's little candle is lit,
> So that at His fire I must melt like wax.'

There is a unity which runs all through St. Paul's account of the Christian experience. Through faith, he holds, God puts us right with Himself, giving us His peace, and bringing us into fellowship with Christ through a union with Him in the power of His life, death, and resurrection, from which we receive the mind which was in Him.

II. THE EXPERIENCE AND THE DEED

No extended discussion is needed to discuss the significance of the connexion St. Paul finds between the Christian experience and the saving deed of Christ. It is probable that he gives far more attention to the experience than he does to the deed. This fact, as well as the quality of his teaching, is enough to demonstrate the claim that we cannot extract St. Paul's doctrine of the Atonement by considering only what he expressly says about Christ's work upon the Cross. The implications of what he says about the Cross are understood only when we study his account of the experience bound up with it. To mention only a single point: we can see why he approaches so nearly to a doctrine of substitution without affirming it. It was impossible for him, as it is impossible for anyone, to describe a death 'instead of us' when, at the same time, we are to die 'with Him', and also he could not speak of suffering, dying, and rising with Him without presenting Him in His representative ministry as bearing sins, submitting to the judgement of God, and, in so doing, revealing His love. In all this teaching there is an undeniable unity. The one strand which stands outside is the cosmic aspects of Christ's death. But even this, in the language of his time, meets a perennial need, since it contains the assurance of victory over every form of evil. The main thing lacking in St. Paul's doctrine of the Cross is a fuller recognition of Christ's present ministry on high. To this he refers when he speaks of 'Christ Jesus that died, yea rather, that was raised from the dead, who is at the right hand of God, who also makes intercession for us' (Rom. viii. 34). But he does not answer the questions which arise in the modern reader's mind. The Epistle to the

Hebrews and I Jn. ii. 1f. have more to say on this theme; yet even still much is left unsaid. And it may be that a fuller account of this ministry is impossible unless we are willing to employ what has been called 'mythopoetical' language[1] for realities which transcend human experience and thought. We ought to judge the New Testament writers, however, by what they say and teach rather than by their silences, and so judged St. Paul stands out by his greatness as a supreme teacher of the redemptive purpose of God in Christ.

[1] Cf. A. N. Wilder, *New Testament Faith for Today* (1955, New York), p. 64.

V

THE TEACHING OF THE EPISTLE
TO THE HEBREWS

IN order fully to appreciate the teaching of this Epistle more attention than is usual needs to be given to its general character and background.

The author of the Epistle is unknown. From the second century onwards the important Church of Alexandria attributed the Epistle to St. Paul, but was compelled to overcome the difficulties of its style by the theory that the actual writing was the work of St. Luke. The great New Testament scholar Origen concluded his discussion of the problem by saying, 'Who wrote the Epistle, God alone knows the truth'. In the west Tertullian assigned the writing to Barnabas, and the west hesitated long in accepting it. Eventually general recognition was won in the fourth and fifth centuries thanks to the influence of Jerome and Augustine. Modern scholarship is practically unanimous in maintaining that the style and ideas of the Epistle are not those of St. Paul, but is not agreed on the question of authorship. Silas, Luke, Clement of Rome, Apollos, and Priscilla the wife of Aquila have been suggested. The period of composition is probably A.D. 70–80.

The acceptance of non-Pauline authorship is not loss. On the contrary, the basis of New Testament teaching is widened. We see how the doctrine of the Cross presented itself to a cultured Alexandrian teacher with both Greek and Jewish sympathies.

These sympathies of the author are of the greatest importance for the understanding of the Epistle. Well acquainted with the Old Testament sacrificial system, he had drunk deeply at the wells of Philo of Alexandria, a great Jewish scholar strongly influenced by the teaching of Plato. One of the most distinctive features of Plato's philosophy is the idea that things visible are but copies of heavenly realities. Things seen are but temporary and transient; things not seen are eternal. We can perceive the influence of this teaching at every point in the Epistle. Judaism, it is held, belongs to the transient world, Christianity to the world of reality. The Christian lives in the eternal order of things, and apostasy, which was a real danger to the readers of the Epistle, is a return to the transient order.

When we understand this point of view, we can see why the author speaks of the Jewish Law as 'a shadow of the good things to come, not the very image of the things' (Heb. x. 1), and his deduction follows that the Jewish sacrifices 'can never make perfect them that draw nigh'. We can see why he says that 'the copies of the things in the heavens' needed to be cleansed again and again by the Jewish sacrifices, 'but the heavenly things with better sacrifices than these' (Heb. ix. 23). And we are in a position to appreciate one of his great utterances when he goes on to say: 'For Christ entered not into a holy place made with hands, like in pattern to the true, but into heaven itself, now to appear before the face of God for us' (Heb. ix. 24). It is understandable that he says that we have no 'abiding city' on earth, but seek after 'that which is to come' (Heb. xiii. 14), and that he speaks of hope as 'an anchor of the soul', which enters into 'that which is within the veil' (Heb. vi. 19). Into this world of reality, he says, Jesus entered for us 'as a forerunner', 'having become a high priest for ever after the order of Melchizedek' (Heb. vi. 20).

The reference to Melchizedek is perplexing to the modern reader, but it is a point of importance in the writer's argument. He knew that Jesus did not belong to the priestly tribe of Levi, but to the tribe of Judah. His attention was arrested by a reference to an older priesthood in Psa. cx. 4 in the words, 'Thou art a priest for ever, after the order of Melchizedek'. He therefore recalls the story of Melchizedek which is told in Gen. xiv. 18–20. There Melchizedek is described as the 'king of Salem'. Our author points out that his name means 'King of righteousness' and that 'Salem' means 'peace'. According to the ancient story Melchizedek met Abraham when he was returning from the slaughter of the four kings and gave him bread and wine, and Abraham gave to him a tenth of the spoil taken in battle. Melchizedek is described in the narrative as 'priest of God Most High'. It is to this priesthood, our author contends, that Christ belongs. He is 'a priest for ever, after the order of Melchizedek'. Judged by modern standpoints this exposition is artificial, but it is characteristic of Alexandrian methods, and it gives the writer the opportunity of insisting that Christ's priesthood is eternal, which is his main doctrinal concern.

Another point which calls for explanation is the writer's conception of faith. To him faith is confidence in the unseen rather than that personal dependence upon Christ which St. Paul describes. As he says in Heb. xi. 1, 'Faith is the substance of things hoped for', or as J. H. Moulton interprets the passage, 'the title-deeds of things hoped for'; it is the assurance that we can claim them.

These points are necessary to the understanding of the Epistle, and it is for this reason that they are mentioned here.

II. THE TEACHING OF THE EPISTLE TO THE HEBREWS WITH REFERENCE TO THE CROSS

I now pass on to describe the leading ideas which the author associates with the Cross. His main emphasis lies upon its vicarious, representative, and sacrificial aspects, and its abiding and eternal significance. Other aspects, its connexion with the divine purpose, its Messianic character, its relation to the love of God,[1] its climax in the Resurrection,[2] and its relation to the idea of the Suffering Servant,[3] receive little attention; and there is no reference at all to the experience of faith union with the Crucified, to sacramental communion, and to teaching concerning suffering with Christ. As we shall see, these omissions are costly, but it is of first importance to see what the writer actually teaches.

His teaching reflects an austere, but majestic conception of God. God, he insists, who in varied parts and ways spoke to the fathers in the prophets, has now spoken to us in His Son. He is the living God, before whom all things are naked and laid open. He is the Judge of men. 'It is a fearful thing', he says, 'to fall into the hands of the living God' (x. 31). He is to be approached with reverence and awe, for He is 'a consuming fire' (xii. 29). Perhaps this is a note we need today, for here is described no benign indulgent Buddha. Nevertheless, we are far from the fulness of New Testament teaching, for nothing is said of the love and the Fatherhood of God.[4]

In view of the central importance which the writer assigns to the work of Christ it is necessary to notice the significance he gives to His person. Great epithets are applied to Him. He is 'the heir of all things', 'the

[1] But see ii. 9, 'that by the grace of God he should taste death for every man'.

[2] Cf. xiii. 20.   [3] Cf. ix. 28.   [4] Apart from ii. 9.

radiance of (God's) glory', 'the impress of his essence' (i. 2f.). But at the same time great stress is laid upon His humanity. He was tempted in all points like as we are, yet without sin (iv. 15). He offered up prayers and supplications 'with strong crying and tears', was heard 'for his godly fear', and, although He was a Son, He yet 'learned obedience by the things which he suffered' (v. 7f.). He is 'the pioneer of salvation', the 'forerunner', the 'mediator of a better covenant'. It has often been pointed out how frequently the human name 'Jesus' is held back by the writer for emphasis. For example, we read, 'We behold him who hath been made a little lower than the angels, *even Jesus*' (ii. 9).

This double emphasis upon the divinity and the humanity of Christ is the necessary basis for all that the writer has to say of His work.

How, then, does he describe the work of Christ?

1. *First, Christ's work is described as a work 'for us'*; it is a vicarious ministry. He was crowned with glory and honour 'that by the grace of God he should taste death *for every man*' (ii. 9). It is as 'a forerunner', the writer says, that Jesus 'entered *for us*' within the veil (vi. 20). His present ministry is 'to appear before the face of God *for us*'. In all passages of this kind the preposition translated 'for' means literally 'on our behalf', not 'instead of us', as in the New Testament generally. He acts 'on our behalf' and 'for every man'.

2. *Secondly, in His atoning ministry Christ represents us*. This idea is implied in all the passages just quoted. This is also true of some nine passages in which Jesus is called our 'high priest'. For example, He is described as 'a merciful and faithful high priest in things pertaining to God' (ii. 17), 'the Apostle and High Priest of our confession' (iii. 1), and 'a high priest of the good things to come' (ix. 11). What lies behind this language?

Our author is thinking of the great Day of Atonement which is the subject of Lev. xvi. Once a year on this day the Levitical high priest offered sacrifice first for himself and then for the sins of the people whom he represented. He then entered into the holy place within the veil, and, having sprinkled the mercy seat with blood, he made atonement for the sins of the people. The writer speaks of this ritual as 'a parable for the time now present' (ix. 9). He then continues:

'But Christ having come a high priest of the good things to come, through the greater and more perfect tabernacle, not made with hands, that is to say, not of this creation, nor yet through the blood of goats and calves, but *through his own blood*, entered in once for all into the holy place, *having obtained eternal redemption*' (ix. 11f.).

He then argues,

'For if the blood of goats and bulls, and the ashes of a heifer sprinkling them that have been defiled, sanctify unto the cleanness of the flesh: how much more shall *the blood of Christ*, who through the eternal Spirit *offered himself without blemish unto God*, cleanse your conscience from dead works to serve the living God?' (ix. 13f.).

We are being asked today to 'demythologize' the New Testament.[1] We must be careful in the process lest in interpreting images we lose realities, but it is certainly right to express biblical teaching in terms which can be understood by modern men. In the passage I have quoted the writer appears to be 'demythologizing' the Old Testament. How shall we attempt to do the same with his own statement? What does it mean? This, I suggest: that, when we draw near to God, there is One who represents us, who speaks for us, as the high priest is said to have done on the Day of Atonement. He has done all things necessary for our salvation. He makes Himself our voice when otherwise we are dumb.

[1] By Rudolf Bultmann in his essay, 'New Testament and Mythology', printed in *Kerygma and Myth*, edited by H. W. Bartsch.

3. *Thirdly, our author teaches, Christ's work consists in the sacrifice of Himself.* There can be no doubt that this is the teaching of the Epistle. Note the phrases which stand out in the long passage I have already quoted: 'through his own blood', 'having obtained eternal redemption', 'the blood of Christ', 'who . . . offered himself'. All this is sacrificial terminology. And, in addition, there are many quite explicit statements in the Epistle. When Jesus is said to be 'a merciful and faithful high priest', His work is explained by the phrase: 'to make expiation for the sins of the people' (ii. 17), that is, to cover sins, so that they no longer are a barrier between ourselves and God. Still more explicitly, we read, 'But now once at the end of the ages hath he been manifested to put away sin *by the sacrifice of himself*' (ix. 26). There are other passages of the kind in the Epistle. The writer's teaching is that Christ is the One Sacrifice for sin.

Again we ask, What does the writer mean? Here and there in the Epistle luminous hints are given. For example, he speaks of the conscience being cleansed 'from dead works to serve the living God' (ix. 14). That is, I take it, a new principle is set up in us, so that, instead of making claims upon God, we are content to be obedient to Him. Or again, in the one allusion to the idea of the Suffering Servant, when he says that Christ has been offered 'to bear the sins of many', that is to say, He bore upon His heart the consequences of human sin (ix. 28). But he does not work out these ideas. In fact, he nowhere tells us how Christ is the One Sacrifice for sin. We are left to think out for ourselves the question, in what way Christ is 'the organ'[1] of our approach to God. Why is this so?

I have attempted to explain this silence elsewhere,[2]

---

[1] This phrase is used by H. H. Rowley in *The Unity of the Bible*, p. 45.
[2] In *The Atonement in New Testament Teaching*, pp. 126–30.

and here refer to two points only. First, the writer could assume that his readers were familiar with sacrificial ideas. 'According to the law', he writes, 'I may almost say, all things are cleansed with blood, and apart from the shedding of blood there is no remission' (ix. 22). He could take this principle for granted, as a belief common to his readers and himself. They knew, as he knew, that 'blood' is the vehicle of surrendered life, and that its shedding was the prescribed way of approach to God. He had, therefore, only to show that the death of Christ was the one supreme Sacrifice to be immediately understood. We to-day are not in their situation. We tend to think of sacrifice in pagan terms, as a means of appeasing the anger of God or as a gift to secure His favour, with the result that for us sacrifice appears to be an outworn religious observance. The writer seems to be saying this very thing, when he declares, 'It is impossible that the blood of bulls and goats should take away sins' (x. 4). In these words, however, he is speaking of the Levitical sacrifices, which are only copies of heavenly realities. He thinks the very opposite of the Sacrifice of Christ which, in his view, avails eternally. He is not able to help us because we live in a different intellectual world. On our part, we have to make an effort to think of Christ's self-offering as one with which we must identify ourselves in faith and in worship as the means of our approach to a reconciling God.

Secondly, the writer's failure to dwell upon the ideas of faith union, suffering with Christ, and sacramental communion, as well as of teaching concerning the love of God, limits his treatment of the One Sacrifice. We have seen how powerfully these ideas bear upon St. Paul's account of the saving deed of Christ. The writer of Hebrews suffers from his restraint. It is true that the

E

Epistle is the only letter we have from his pen. Yet it is hard to think that he could have omitted to speak of them if they had been living in his thinking. The lesson is plain. One cannot omit these ideas without loss to the theology of the Atonement. Without them the One Sacrifice stands apart, solitary in its sublimity. If they are living, the Sacrifice is one in which we have part, one which we can make our own in drawing near in penitence to God. The Sacrifice is always His, but in a true sense it becomes ours also. In this situation we see the true unity of New Testament teaching, namely that elements prominent in one teacher are supplemented by those emphasized by another.

4. *Fourthly, in addition to the ideas already mentioned, the writer powerfully describes the eternal ministry of Christ on high,* His Session at the right hand of God. This idea, which is found also in the Acts, the Pauline Epistles, and the Apocalypse, as well as in the teaching of Jesus Himself, is based on Psa. cx. 1,

'The Lord saith unto my lord,
Sit thou at my right hand,
Until I make thine enemies thy footstool.'

This Psalm is frequently quoted in the Epistle. The writer affirms that, when Jesus had made purification for sins, He 'sat down on the right hand of the Majesty on high' (i. 3). The same claim is made in viii. 1, in x. 12, and in xii. 2. It is a point of vital importance to his theology. The phrase presents Jesus as Victor, as Ruler, as Helper, and as Advocate. The ministry specially emphasized by the writer is that of intercession, for, after affirming that Christ's priesthood is 'unchangeable', he writes: 'Wherefore also he is able to save to the utter-most them that draw near unto God through him, seeing he ever lives to make intercession for them' (vii. 25). We are reminded of St. Paul's words in Rom. viii. 34 and of St. John's declaration, 'We have an Advocate with the Father, Jesus Christ the righteous' (I Jn. ii. 1).

Here we have an idea which is making an increasing appeal to Christians of to-day, as the popularity of Jean Ingelow's hymn, 'And didst Thou love the race that loved not Thee?', testifies, especially the line, 'Art Thou his kinsman now?' There is another hymn of like character, which John Wesley in his *Journal* tells us was sung by John Lancaster and his nine companions on their way to execution. They were visited daily by Sarah Peters, who pointed them to God, and as they journeyed to Tyburn they sang Charles Wesley's hymn:

> 'Lamb of God, whose bleeding love
> We still recall to mind,
> Send the answer from above,
> And let us mercy find.'

> 'Think on us, who think on Thee,
> And every struggling soul release:
> O remember Calvary:
> And let us go in peace!'

As we saw in the first lecture this ceaseless ministry of Christ is an essential part of the doctrine of the Atonement. It is the peculiar merit of the Epistle to the Hebrews that it affirms its reality so impressively. The nature of Christ's intercession, which it need hardly be said implies no reluctance to be overcome on the part of God, is not described by the writer, and it remains a theme for adoring meditation. We may believe that it voices the unutterable in the contrition and penitence of man.

VI

THE TEACHING OF ST. JOHN

IT is often claimed that in a well-used Bible there is no
part so well thumbed as the fourteenth chapter of St.
John's Gospel. The familiar story regarding Sir
Walter Scott illustrates this claim. When he lay dying
at Abbotsford he asked his son-in-law Lockhart to read
to him. When Lockhart asked what he should read,
Scott replied, 'Need you ask? there is but one book', and
Lockhart read Jn. xiv, 'Let not your heart be troubled . . .'.

It is perhaps unfortunate that Jn. xiv has tened tod
foster the delusion that John is a simple Gospel, easy to
understand. It is simple so long as you take it as it
stands, asking no questions. But it is anything but
simple, if you consider its outstanding features—the
differences between it and Mark, Matthew, and Luke,
the author's masterful attitude to history, his choice of
themes, the new idiom in which he presents the sayings
of Jesus, what he includes and what he omits.

The Gospel is an interpretation, an inspired interpretation, of the person of Christ. This fact explains the
author's emphasis on doctrine and his selection of
narratives. He is not indifferent to history; he firmly
believes that 'the Word became flesh' (i. 14); but the
kind of factual history to which the modern historian
attaches so much importance does not interest him.
What does it mean, this manifestation of the Word in
flesh? This is his preoccupation. 'These things are
written', he says, 'that you may believe that Jesus is the

Christ, the Son of God, and that believing you may have life in his name' (xx. 31).

St. John is the latest of the Gospels and was written probably in the last decade of the first century. The traditional view is that it was written by the Apostle John the son of Zebedee, but this theory is largely abandoned by modern New Testament scholars, although many believe that his testimony lies behind it. Whoever the author was, his mind was steeped in Old Testament teaching, in rabbinical speculation, and in Greek religious ideas concerning life, light, and the conflict between light and darkness, life and death, truth and error. On rather slight evidence some scholars think that he was a member of the Essene sect whose writings have recently been found in the caves of Qumran by the Dead Sea. Others trace his debt to the writings of Philo, the Alexandrian scholar already mentioned who sought to interpret the Old Testament in the light of Greek philosophy, others again to the Baptist sect known as the Mandaeans, and others to Gnosticism, that strange religious movement which emphasized the importance of knowledge, the evil of matter, and the descent of saviours from the realms of light. Some of these influences may have played their part, but the impression I receive is that he was responsive to Jewish and Greek ideas which were *in the air*, just as evolution and existentialism are known to-day, and that they influenced his presentation of Jesus as the divine Work or Logos of God. The deepest motive was his knowledge of the tradition of the Church of his day and his own experience of life in fellowship with the Risen and Exalted Christ. The Gospel and the First Epistle are attributed to different authors by some scholars. If this view is accepted, the basis of New Testament teaching is widened. I believe that, in spite of differences of language and thought, they are the work of the same writer and that, in consequence, we learn more about his theology from the two writings.

St. John's characteristic teaching concerning the Cross can be seen both in his treatment of traditional ideas and in his more distinctive thoughts. I propose, therefore, to discuss both aspects of his teaching.

II. ST. JOHN'S USE OF THE TEACHING HE RECEIVED

We see the characteristic Johannine note if we consider the manner in which he presents the Cross as the fulfilment of the divine purpose.

He strongly emphasizes this idea of purpose. The Son of Man 'must be lifted up' as Moses lifted up the serpent in the wilderness (iii. 14). The Father loves the Son because He lays down His life (x. 17). Jesus speaks of His 'hour' (xii. 23, xvii. 1). At Cana of Galilee he says, 'My hour is not yet come' (ii. 4). The Evangelist speaks of the failure to arrest Jesus in the same way, 'No man laid hands on him, because his hour was not yet come' (vii. 30). In the highpriestly prayer Jesus cries, 'Father, the hour is come' (xvii. 1). He also speaks of His 'time'. Thus, to His brothers he says, 'My time is not yet come, but your time is always ready' (vii. 6). A sense of divine destiny marks all that He says concerning His death and exaltation. So also in I John we read, 'We have beheld and bear witness that the Father hath sent the Son to be the Saviour of the world' (iv. 14).

1. This divine purpose is one of love. 'God so loved the world that he gave his only-begotten Son, that whosoever believes in him should not perish, but have eternal life' (iii. 16). So again in I John, 'Herein is love,

not that we loved God, but that he loved us, and sent his Son to be the expiation for our sins' (iv. 10).

2. It is a purpose which meets man's need. The good shepherd lays down His life 'for the sheep' (x. 11). 'Greater love has no man than this, that a man lays down his life for his friends' (xv. 13). Caiaphas is made to say, 'It is expedient for you that one man should die for the people' (xi. 50). This is a striking example of what has been called the Evangelist's 'dramatic irony'. Once more the same idea is found in I John: 'Hereby know we love, because he laid down his life for us' (iii. 16).

3. The purpose is that of taking away sins. 'Behold', cries the Baptist, 'the Lamb of God, who takes away the sin of the world' (i. 29). The parallel in I John is 'You know that he was manifested to take away sins' (iii. 5). He is 'the expiation for our sins; and not for ours only, but also for the whole world' (ii. 2).

4. Positively expressed, the purpose is that of imparting life in its fulness. I content myself here with well-known phrases: 'that whosoever believes may in him have eternal life' (iii. 15); 'that whosoever believes in him should not perish, but have eternal life' (iii. 16). Side by side with these I set the passage in I John which says that God sent His only-begotten Son 'that we might live through him' (iv. 9).

5. The fulfilment of the purpose is expressed in sacrificial language. Examples in the Gospel are the name 'the Lamb of God' (i. 29), the sayings about eating the flesh and drinking the blood of the Son of Man (vi. 53–6), the imagery of the grain of wheat which falls into the ground, dies, and bears much fruit (xii. 24), the allegory of 'the True Vine' (xv. 1–10), and the saying, 'And on their behalf I sanctify myself, that they also may be sanctified in truth' (xvii. 19). The first

Epistle is even more explicit. It speaks of 'the blood of Jesus his Son' which 'cleanses us from all sin' (i. 7). It uses the names 'Advocate' (ii. 1) and 'Expiation' (ii. 2), and, as we have seen, declares that Christ was manifested 'to take away sins' (iii. 5).

Such are the ways in which St. John lays his stamp on primitive Christian ideas. In all this he is selective, for there are other ideas which he does not mention. He has no teaching, comparable to that of the Epistle to the Hebrews, about the One Sacrifice, no allusions, as in I Peter and the Pauline Epistles, to sin-bearing, no mention of dying with Christ,[1] no reference to the Suffering Servant of the Lord (unless it be in i. 29),[2] no sayings, as in St. Mark and St. Paul, which suggest the idea of sharing in the redemptive power of Christ's Sacrifice. Even in I John Jesus does not 'make expiation'; He Himself is 'the Expiation' (ii. 2).

The reason for this selective and distinctive use of the tradition is that in St. John's mind everything is concentrated upon the Person of Christ. For him the Atonement and the Incarnation stand in the closest possible connexion. This fact will appear more clearly still if we consider his most distinctive teaching about the death of Christ.

III. ST. JOHN'S MOST DISTINCTIVE TEACHING

This teaching, to which we now turn, includes two great ideas: (1) the death of Christ as His glorifying, and (2) as His victory over the Prince of Evil.

1. *Glorifying.* The Evangelist sees the glory of God in the earthly life of Christ (i. 14, 'We beheld his glory'),

---

[1] He speaks, however, repeatedly of 'being in Christ' and of 'abiding in Him'. See *Forgiveness and Reconciliation*, pp. 119–22.

[2] He quotes Isa. liii 1 in xii. 38, but not in relation to the death of Christ.

but he knows that this glory is confined by the conditions
of His human lot. Thus, on earth, the Johannine Christ
'groans in spirit' and is 'troubled' (xi. 33, 38), and He
declares to His disciples that it is 'expedient' that He
should 'go away' from them (xvi. 7). In contrast, when
the Greeks ask to see Him, He cries, 'The hour is come
that the Son of Man should be glorified' (xii. 23), and
when Judas goes out into the night to betray Him, He
exults, 'Now is the Son of Man glorified, and God is
glorified in him' (xiii. 31f.). Death and glorifying are
identified. This view explains the ambiguity of the
phrase 'lifted up' in the Gospel. Commentators debate
whether it refers to crucifixion or exaltation. In fact
both are included, as, for example, in the saying, 'I, if I
be lifted up from the earth, will draw all men unto
myself' (xii. 32). He will draw all men to Himself
because He is glorified and exalted in death.

2. *Judgement.* John has no doubt about the existence
of the Devil, or, as he calls him 'the Prince of this world'.
In his view the coming of Christ is a decisive conflict
with the powers of darkness. His glorifying in death is
therefore a sentence of judgement. Thus, before speaking of being 'lifted up', He cries, 'Now is the judgement
of this world: now shall the Prince of this world be
cast out' (xii. 31). Jewish expectation saw the casting
down of Satan as an event in the last times, that is, as an
eschatological event: St. John sees it as present, as
implicit in the glorifying of Christ. In the Upper Room
Jesus says, 'The Prince of this world comes, and has
nothing in me' (xiv. 30), and He prophesies that the
Paraclete, the Holy Spirit, will convict the world of
judgement, as well as of sin and of righteousness, 'because
the Prince of this world has been judged' (xvi. 11).

The First Epistle does not mention glorifying, but it

speaks directly of judgement: 'To this end was the Son of God manifested, that he might destroy the works of the devil' (iii. 8). The Incarnation, consummated in death, is the virtual destruction of evil. Satan is a beaten foe, all the more terrible because he lies under the sentence of death. So without contradiction the writer can say, 'We know that we are of God, and the whole world lies in the evil one' (v. 19).

In sum, one cannot fail to see that, whether the Evangelist recasts traditional teaching, or whether he presents his more distinctive teaching, the governing idea is that of victory utter and complete through death. Throughout he is preoccupied with the Person and Work of Christ.

IV. THE RESULTS OF THE EVANGELIST'S VIEWS

In the light of the Evangelist's theology many distinctive features in the Johannine writings are explained.

1. We see why he lays such emphasis upon faith as believing in Christ Himself. As a matter of fact, he never uses the noun 'faith', doubtless because it was being misapplied in Gnostic circles. And there is only a single example in the Epistle (v. 4). He prefers to use the verb 'to believe', and he has it about one hundred times. Of these thirty-four in the Gospel and three in the Epistle are used with the preposition 'into' or 'in', a construction which, as J. H. Moulton[1] says, recalls that mystical union St. Paul describes by the phrase 'in Christ'. The Evangelist also speaks of 'being in Christ' and 'abiding in Christ', but, as we have seen, not of suffering with Christ or of sharing in His Sacrifice. It is wrong, I think, to set one cycle of ideas over against the other,

---

[1] *Grammar of New Testament Greek, Prolegomena*, p. 68.

still more to suppose that the one excludes the other. The difference arises from the Evangelist's dominant interest in the Incarnation.

2. This interest accounts for the character of St. John's Passion Narrative. His narrative lacks the more human traits of St. Mark's account. It omits, for example, the Gethsemane story, or rather the Evangelist recasts the narrative and introduces it at an earlier point in his Gospel, cancelling much of its pathos. 'Now is my soul troubled, and what shall I say?', asks the Johannine Christ, 'Shall I say, Father, save me from this hour?[1] But for this cause came I to this hour' (xii. 27). In the Passion Narrative itself it is replaced by words addressed to the impetuous Peter, when he cuts off the right ear of Malchus, 'The cup which the Father has given me, shall I not drink it?' (xviii. 11). When Judas and the Roman soldiers seek Jesus, He answers with His majestic 'I am he', whereupon all fall to the ground (xviii. 6). The high priest who asks concerning His teaching, is answered with the greatest boldness, 'Why do you ask me, ask them that heard me, what I spoke unto them' (xviii. 21), so that the officers strike Him (xviii. 22).

Jesus judges His judges. When Pilate asks, 'Are you a king?', Jesus replies, 'To this end have I been born, and to this end came I into the world, that I should bear witness to the truth' (xviii. 37). When Pilate asks, 'Whence are you?', Jesus is silent, and when the governor speaks of his power to release or to crucify, He says, 'You would have no power against me, except it were given to you from above' (xix. 11). Pilate presents Jesus to the Jews with the provocative words, 'Behold, your King!', and with satire they are made to reply, 'We have no king but Caesar' (xix. 15). The inscription, 'Jesus of

---

[1] The words are probably a question, not a statement.

Nazareth, the King of the Jews', is set upon the cross in
Hebrew, Latin, and Greek, and Pilate refuses to alter it
saying, 'What I have written, I have written' (xix. 22).
When Jesus receives the wine, He cries *Tetelestai*, 'It is
finished', and chooses to die. Unlike St. Mark St. John does
not say that Jesus 'expired' (Mk. xv. 37, cf. Lk. xxii. 46),
but that 'bending his head, he gave up his spirit' (xix. 30).

All the way through Jesus is in command. The Cross
is His throne. The narrative is one of theological interpretation. And we must welcome this interpretation, for
we see who this Man is who consents to die. He is the
King of the Ages, who makes the Cross a stairway to
heaven. The same notes run through the Resurrection
narratives. They reach their climax in the words,
'Blessed are they who have not seen, and yet have believed'
(xx. 29), and in the declaration that 'these things are
written, that you may believe that Jesus is the Christ the
Son of God, and that believing you may have life in his
name' (xx. 31).

3. This marked Christological interest goes far to
explain the differences between the Gospel and the First
Epistle. We have seen that the traditional aspects of the
doctrine of the Cross are more prominent in the Epistle.
The explanation may be that the Epistle is the later
writing. Brilliant theologians not infrequently find a
new interest in tradition as they grow older. But the
better explanation probably is that the dominating
interest in the Person of Christ, although prominent also
in the Epistle, is less in control. Pastoral interests super-
vene, and the Cross is seen in its own light.

v. THE VALUE OF ST. JOHN'S TEACHING

1. First, its value lies in the new impress it gives to
older teaching. This impress is seen in the Evangelist's

emphasis on love and on life. The Cross reveals the love of God which, as Abelard taught, awakens an answering response in the heart of man: 'God so loved the world'. St. Paul says much the same in Rom. v. 8, but St. John stamps it upon the mind. So also he stresses the idea of life in the words, 'that whosoever believes on him may have eternal life' (iii. 16).

2. Secondly its value shines out in the distinctive teaching about glorifying and judgement. Both St. Paul and St. John speak of the saving deed of Christ, but in St. John it is pre-eminently *Christ's deed*. St. Paul had said that God set forth Christ 'as a means of expiation' (*hilasterion*). St. John had reflected on this teaching, but he puts it in a new way. 'Yes', he says in effect, 'but *He* is the Expiation' (*hilasmos*). He is what He does. St. John turns St. Paul's adjective into a noun which describes Christ's Person.

There is no exact parallel to this usage, but there are many analogies. We speak of 'a Turner', but we mean one of his pictures. We say, 'I am reading Browning'. We mean we are reading *A Death in the Desert*, *Bishop Blougram's Apology*, or *The Ring and the Book*. We speak of Shakespeare, when we mean *Macbeth* or *Julius Caesar*. We identify the work with the man. Sometimes this way of speaking applies to nations. Britain's 'finest hour' was Britain; 'lease-lend' was America. So St. John: 'Now is the Son of Man glorified'; 'He is the Expiation'. The gibbet becomes a face; the Cross a Person. Similarly St. John transforms the idea of Judgement. It becomes an activity, not a court. He does not pass sentence upon Satan. Satan falls because Christ is King. The Cross is a crown and therefore the cause of crisis, a sceptre which decides the fate of evil.

3. Finally, the glory of this teaching is its place in the

unity of New Testament teaching. We are not to isolate it, not to treat it as the whole. St. John does not cancel out St. Paul, nor St. Paul St. John. We welcome the truth that the Cross is Christ *in excelsis*; but we still need the knowledge that it is Christ's saving deed, that He bears sins, represents us before God, and gives us a share in His Sacrifice. St. John's teaching rings out like a trumpet, but the place for a trumpet is within the divine orchestra. Here, together with the heart-moving strains of St. Paul, the diapason notes of Hebrews, the liturgical echoes of St. Peter, we hear the Johannine peal of victory. 'Herein is love, not that we loved God, but that he loved us, and sent his Son to be the expiation[1] for our sins (I Jn. iv. 10).

[1] In all cases I have used in these Johannine passages, instead of 'propitiation', the rendering 'expiation' in the sense of 'covering' sins, or 'making atonement' for them.

VII

MODERN THEORIES OF THE ATONEMENT

NEXT to the study of Scripture there is perhaps no better way of approaching the meaning of the Cross than by examining the outstanding discussions of the doctrine during the last century. We can see how the problems presented themselves to the minds of learned theologians, the ideas which fell by the way, and the fruitful developments which were made possible. Such an inquiry can be dull, if no more than a catalogue of opinions is attempted, but it can also be full of interest if the main points are brought out and presented to the reader. I discovered this fact during the Second World War, at Keswick, in the English Lake District, when, in response to the request of a number of American chaplains, I discussed the great books which have been written on the Atonement. I shall, of course, have to make my own selection, and the problem is to know what to include and what to omit. I shall begin with the year 1856 and end with 1935. Later books must be given time to find their place, but older classical discussions can never safely be neglected.

1. It will be useful first to mention, for purposes of reference, the *four main types*, which in various forms have persisted throughout the centuries. The oldest theory is the *'Ransom Theory'*, the view that Christ died to rescue men from the power of sin, death, and Satan. It held sway for a thousand years. In the hands of some of the

Fathers it assumed strange forms as when, for example, the Cross was described as a mousetrap baited with the blood of Christ. We must not allow ourselves to be revolted by crudities of this kind. The value of this theory was that it emphasized the immense cost of redemption and the reality of evil. In recent times it has been revived and restated by G. Aulén and S. Cave.

2. The second classical theory is the '*Satisfaction Theory*' put forward by Anselm in the eleventh century. Presented against a background of feudalism, it suggests that Christ died to 'satisfy' the wounded honour of God. In its doctrine of forgiveness it is deficient, but it rightly insists that in the atoning work of Christ there are divine conditions which must be met if 'satisfaction' is to be ethical. Again and again the charge is pressed, 'Not yet hast thou considered how great is the weight of sin'.

3. Abelard's '*Theory of Revelation*', sometimes described as the 'Moral Influence Theory', followed that of Anselm in the early part of the twelfth century. Its substance is well expressed in the words of Peter Lombard, 'So great a pledge of love having been given to us, we are both moved and kindled to love God who did such great things for us. The death of Christ therefore justifies us, inasmuch as through it charity is stirred up in our hearts'. This truth is the presupposition of any worthy doctrine of the Atonement. Whether it is adequate is another matter.

4. The '*Forensic Theory*' is that of the Reformers and their successors. It is the view that Christ suffered the judgement of God upon sin in our stead. It is 'substitutionary' in character, and therefore open to challenge. But it powerfully preserves the idea that Christ did for us what we cannot do for ourselves and that His righteousness is open to our taking.

Besides these ideas the Greek Fathers often spoke of atonement as a work of deification, and at all times emphasis has been laid upon sacrificial concepts.

It is against the background of these great historical theories that I wish to describe the contributions of modern theologians.

II. THE VIEWS OF TEN MODERN THEOLOGIANS

1. *J. McLeod Campbell* (*The Nature of the Atonement*, 1856). Today McLeod Campbell is justly recognized as one of the greatest theologians of Scotland or indeed of any land. He has been described by J. H. Leckie as 'the greatest theological genius of his day'.[1] Deposed by the Church of Scotland in 1831, when he was thirty-one years of age, because he taught the universality of the Atonement and the doctrine of Assurance, he formed no new sect. He ministered to his own congregation in Glasgow until 1859, and on his retirement he advised its members to return to the national Church. His book is not easy to read because of the prolixity of its style. 'Man', his father wrote to him, 'you have a queer way of putting things'. His sermons, on the contrary, are lucid in expression. Nevertheless *The Nature of the Atonement* contains many passages of great beauty and power. Although written a century ago, it is still a classic work of theology.

Campbell rejects the idea of vicarious punishment and his position is best given in his own words:

'Let my reader endeavour to realize the thought. The *sufferer suffers* what he suffers *just through seeing sin and sinners with God's eyes, and feeling in reference to them with God's heart.* Is *such* suffering *a punishment?* . . . There can be but one answer . . . I find myself shut up to the conclusion, that while Christ suffered

---

[1] *The Expository Times*, xl. 198–204.

F

for our sins as an atoning sacrifice, what He suffered was not—
because from its nature it could not be—a punishment.'[1]

Taking a hint from Jonathan Edwards,[2] Campbell
develops the idea that Christ, as the representative and
complete man, was able to offer a vicarious repentance to
God for men.

'This confession', he writes, 'as to its own nature must
have been a perfect Amen in humanity to the judgement
of God on the sin of man.'[3]   To this confession of Christ
our own 'Amen' is faith.

'Our faith is, in truth, the Amen of our individual spirits to that
deep, multiform, all-embracing, harmonious Amen of humanity,
in the person of the Son of God, to the mind and heart of the
Father in relation to man—the divine wrath and the divine mercy,
which is the atonement.'[4]

The common objection to this view is that it replaces
a legal by a moral fiction.   Only the sinner, it is objected,
can repent.   No one, not even Christ, can repent for us.
To a reviewer Campbell pointed out that he had no
thought of suggesting a *substituted* repentance, and he
argues that Christ's offering was accepted by the Father
entirely with the prospective purpose that it is to be
reproduced in us.

It is significant that, while few have accepted Campbell's
theory, as it stands, few have been able to ignore it.   We
shall see that something like it reappears in R. C.
Moberly's *Atonement and Personality*.   Moberly suggested
that the results might have been different, if Campbell
had been born and bred in a Catholic atmosphere, with

[1] *Op. cit.*, p. 117.   The italics are Campbell's.

[2] Leckie reminds us that Edwards had said that, if it had been possible
for man to have offered to God the sacrifice of a perfect confession and
repentance, that would have been atonement enough for sin, *op. cit.*, 201.

[3] *Op. cit.*, p. 135.   [4] *Op. cit.*, p. 194.

its emphasis upon sacramental communion. Scotsmen will be slow to accept this suggestion, but it is worth pondering.

2. *H. Bushnell* (*The Vicarious Sacrifice*, 1866). Ten years later this great American theologian published his well-known book. He too was viewed with much suspicion in his day, but there can be no doubt about his greatness. He is often described as an Abelardian, but there is much more in his teaching than an appeal to the moral influence of Christ's death.

Bushnell rejects with vigour the theory that Christ died to satisfy the divine justice. He strongly maintains that, both in His life and His death, Christ is the Moral Power of God. Thus far, he is Abelardian, as we all are. But he also speaks of Christ's death as a sacrifice which is much more than a revelation of God. The Cross, he affirms, is *in God*. He writes:

'Nay, if we will let our plummet down to the bottom of this great sea, the cross of Jesus represents and reveals the tremendous cross that is hid in the bosom of God's love and life from all eternity.'[1]

As quoted in the first lecture he affirms that 'there is a cross in God before the wood is seen upon Calvary, hid in God's own virtue itself'.

His teaching contains hints and suggestions of other ideas. While rejecting the doctrine of penal substitution, he was haunted by the thought that elements of essential value lay behind what he rejected, and in *Forgiveness and Law* (1874) he sought to do justice to them.

In *The Vicarious Sacrifice* he speaks of Christ as 'my sacrifice, who opens all to me'. 'Beholding Him with all my sin upon Him', he says, 'I count Him my offering, I come to God by Him and enter into the Holiest by His

[1] *Op. cit.*, p. 259.

blood.'[1] Bushnell was a preacher-theologian and a theologian for preachers.

3. *R. W. Dale* (*The Atonement*, 1875). Nine years later in Dale we come to another preacher-theologian. Indeed, from Augustine onwards the greatest theologians have been preachers. And not without reason, for 'the heart makes the theologian'. Dale's book is steeped in biblical teaching. He wrestles, not too successfully, with the problem of penal satisfaction, with the strongest desire to meet its ethical difficulties. Let us see how he deals with this question, for it is folly to evade it.

Dale argues that Christ died to meet the demands of 'the Law of Righteousness', a law which is 'alive in God', he says, and which requires that sin must be punished. If its penalties are to be remitted, he contends, some other divine act 'of at least equal intensity' must take its place.[2] Again, we are reminded of Jonathan Edwards.[3] Is there such an act? Dale suggests that it is provided when Christ *Himself* endures penal suffering. He is not satisfied, however, to think of His suffering as an external transaction self-operative in itself, and for this reason he dwells on the fact of an original and ideal relation which exists between Christ and the human race. We are bound up with Him. 'We truly live only as we live in Christ.[4]' He writes:

'By no fictitious imputation or technical transfer, but by virtue of a real union between the life of Christ and our own life, His relation to the Father becomes ours.'[5]

In Dale's teaching we see two significant trends in the theology of the time, the idea of Christ's representative relationship to man and the doctrine of union with Christ on the part of the believing man. Dale's theology is

---

[1] *Op. cit.*, p. 461. [2] *Op. cit.*, 391. [3] See the footnote on p. 74.
[4] *Op. cit.*, 419. [5] *Op. cit.*, 420.

an uneasy combination of the old and the new. New shoots begin to appear in the theological tree. It is of the greatest interest to observe how this combination of ideas is worked out in later writers.

4. *John Scott Lidgett* (*The Spiritual Principle of the Atonement*, 1897). Towards the close of the century Lidgett wrote a great work which stands in line with the best theological tradition. Lidgett was a Methodist writer, perhaps the greatest Methodist theologian of any period, although he himself would have awarded this palm to William B. Pope. He died comparatively recently at the great age of ninety-eight. His Gladstonian eloquence, expressed in long sustained sentences, is that of an older day. A theologian, a preacher of great power, and an ecclesiastical statesman of acknowledged ability, he was profoundly interested in ecumenical Christianity and especially in the question of Church Reunion. His deepest theological interest was in the doctrine of the Fatherhood of God and is embodied in a volume which bears that title. In his *Spiritual Principle* he seeks to combine this doctrine, as indicated in its sub-title, with the idea of the Atonement as 'a Satisfaction made to God for the Sins of the World'.

'Our Lord', he writes, 'in His death fulfilled all the conditions of filial satisfaction. He "tasted" to the full of those penal conditions which reveal the wrath of God against sin; He made them, by His perfect self-surrender, the means of perfecting His fellowship with the Father, the consummation of His obedience, His homage to that law of righteousness of which sin is the transgression.'[1]

If we ponder these words, we see that the whole question has been lifted out of the law court into the family, but with no attempt to lessen its urgency.

[1] *Op. cit.*, 282.

Lidgett stresses the relationship which exists between Christ and ourselves.

'His relationship to the human race, and His consequent Incarnation, enabled Him, and Him alone, to give complete expression, under our penal conditions, to the submission of mankind to God, to make reparation to His law, and to put away sin from man.'[1]

Those who dismiss the penal aspect of Christ's work, as an outworn conception, ought, I think, to reflect upon the passages I have quoted, and to couple with these a third in which Lidgett speaks of our relationship to Christ. Faith in Christ, he holds, makes His death our sacrifice.

'That which Christ uttered to God in His death, we by faith utter in Him. All that the Cross meant of surrender to God, of honour to the law of righteousness, of repudiation of transgression, becomes by faith the object to which our repentance and consecration are joined, and in which they are perfectly expressed to God.'[2]

In this work one can see a further softening of the hard legal outlines of earlier theories coupled with a resolute endeavour to take serious account of the divine judgement which rests upon sin. A second notable feature is the close relationship described between Christ and man and between the believer and Christ. His work is the service of love and is the medium of our own approach to God.

5. *R. C. Moberly* (*Atonement and Personality,* 1901). At the turn of the century only a brief interval separates Moberly's great work from that of Lidgett. In it there is an even stronger interest in the ethical aspects of the Atonement together with a distinctive emphasis upon sacramental communion and the doctrine of the Holy Spirit. *Atonement and Personality* is a work of great beauty and suggestiveness. Written by an outstanding

---

[1] *Op. cit.*, 378. [2] *Op. cit.*, 407f.

Anglican scholar, it combines subtlety of expression with warmth of religious feeling. It is the work of a theologian, a philosopher, and a worshipper all in one, and is written on so broad a scale that it gives the reader a liberal education in theology in general.

In many respects the argument reminds us of that of McLeod Campbell. Whereas Campbell speaks of Christ's perfect confession of our sins, Moberly attributes to Him the offering of 'the sacrifice of supreme penitence'.

Naturally the objection brought against Campbell's views has been pressed in the case of Moberly. Only the sinner, it is objected, can be penitent. Moberly seeks to meet this objection in three ways. (*a*) He dwells upon the inclusiveness of Christ's humanity. Christ is Man. In Moberly's challenging words, He is 'not generically, but inclusively, man'.[1] Many theologians find this submission hard to accept, since Christ is so clearly represented in the New Testament as a man.[2] (*b*) Further, Moberly maintains that it is only the personally sinless who can be truly penitent, since sin blunts the edge and dims the power of penitence. His illustration is that of the mother who makes the shame of her erring child her own. He says of Christ:

'He did, in fact and in full, that which would in the sinner constitute perfect atonement, but which has for ever become impossible to the sinner, just in proportion as it is true that he has sinned.'[3]

He consummated penitence, he teaches, not that men might be excused from the need of repenting, 'but that they might learn, in Him, their own true possibility of penitence'.[4] (*c*) Again, Moberly strongly insists upon the

---

[1] *Op. cit.*, 86.   Cf. W. P. Du Bose, *The Gospel in the Gospels*, 157.
[2] Cf. Phil. ii. 7, Rom. v. 15, Gal. iv. 4, I Tim. ii. 5.
[3] *Op. cit.*, 130.   [4] *Op. cit.*, 284.

work of the Holy Spirit in the hearts of men, and power-fully expounds the importance of the Church and the Sacraments. The essential thing, he urges, is union with Christ.

'Sacramental communion', he writes, 'is vainly material after all, if it is not conceived of mainly as an aspiration and growing on towards oneness—not mechanically, so much, as of flesh, as inherently of character and spirit, with the Crucified.'[1]

This extension of the personal aspects of faith to its communal expression in worship and sacramental com-munion is a necessary and permanent contribution to the doctrine of the Atonement.

6. *James Denney* (*The Christian Doctrine of Reconcilia-tion*, 1917). Denney's earlier work, *The Death of Christ* (1903), is an invaluable study of New Testament teaching, strongly Pauline in its sympathies and scintillating in expression. His maturest thought, however, is reflected in *The Christian Doctrine of Reconciliation* which was pub-lished after his death. It is to this work, therefore, that we must turn in estimating the contribution of this prince among Scottish theologians to the doctrine of the Atone-ment.

Denney is insistent that full justice must be done to the reality of the moral order in the universe. Thus, he maintains, it is divinely necessary 'that sin, in the very process in which it is forgiven, should also, in all its reality, be borne'.[2] Christ's sufferings, he holds, are penal, but he carefully explains that they have this character, not because Christ Himself was the object of the divine wrath, but in the sense that 'in that dark hour He had to realise to the full the divine reaction against sin in the race in which He was incorporated'.[3] Other-wise, He could not have been the Redeemer and the

---

[1] *Op. cit.*, 271.   [2] *Op. cit.*, 161.   [3] *Op. cit.*, 273.

Reconciler of sinful men to God.   As in the case of many of the theologians whose contributions we are considering, he strongly insists that Christ's work becomes effective through faith.

'Faith', he writes, 'freely and passionately identifies the sinner with the sin-bearer, absorbing into itself all His attitude in relation to sin.'[1]

In few modern theologians is the work of Christ so powerfully described and the nature of faith so clearly indicated, especially when he is expounding Pauline teaching.   Of St. Paul he says, 'It is not historical scholarship that is wanted for an understanding of him, and neither is it the insight of genius: it is despair'.[2]

7. *Hastings Rashdall* (*The Idea of Atonement in Christian Theology*, 1919).   This work is a brilliant statement by a Broad Churchman of the Abelardian view of the Atonement, that is, the theory that the Cross of Christ is the supreme revelation of the Love of God.   In it the substitutionary theory is trenchantly handled, but, in the light of the works already described, one has the feeling that it fights a battle already won.   It fails also to take account of the values which that theory sought to conserve in respect of the divine judgement which undoubtedly rests upon evil and sin.   Like Prince Rupert's cavalry, it wins the charge, but loses the battle.

Rashdall claims that the only doctrine of the Atonement which can be traced back to Christ Himself is 'the simple doctrine that His death, like His life, was one of self-sacrifice for His followers'.[3]   No kind of justice is done to the sayings of Jesus which reflect the influence of the Servant conception of Isa. liii or to the greatness of Pauline teaching.   All the stress lies on the great thought

[1] *Op. cit.*, 305.   [2] *Op. cit.*, 180.   [3] *Op. cit.*, 45.

that the Cross reveals the Love of God, but the question, 'What did the love do and bear?', is neither asked nor answered. It is, I think, significant that R. S. Franks in his book, *The Atonement*, finds it necessary to combine Abelardian teaching with ideas stressed by Anselm in his statement of the doctrine of 'Satisfaction' in *Cur Deus Homo?* The inference would seem to be that if, in our teaching about the Cross, we dwell, as we must, upon the Love of God, and seek to express all that we say in the light of this basic truth, we still need to consider how this Love deals with man in his sinful plight and effects his salvation. Rashdall's discussion underlines the need for a more positive statement.

8. *F. C. N. Hicks* (*The Fullness of Sacrifice*, 1930). A new path was opened by Bishop Hicks in a work which interprets the Atonement in terms of Old Testament ideas of sacrifice and brings the Christian Eucharist into the closest connexion with it. This book is marked by its charity, its insight, and its great spiritual power. The Old Testament sacrifices are viewed as vehicles of expression. The sacrifices are seen in a composite and idealised picture which includes (*a*) the idea of the surrender of life, (*b*) the offering of life so surrendered, and (*c*) the union between God and man sealed by communion in the life transformed by God's acceptance of it. The Eucharist, Bishop Hicks maintains, is 'an integral part, for us on earth, of the One Sacrifice in its fullness'.[1] The book illustrates the growing tendency of many British and continental scholars[2] to bring the sacrament of the Lord's Supper into close association with the doctrine of the Cross. The Body and the Blood, it is argued by Bishop

---

[1] *Op. cit.*, 346.
[2] Cf. R. Otto, *The Kingdom of God and the Son of Man* ; J. Jeremias, *The Eucharistic Sayings of Jesus*, 27, 105.

Hicks, are the Body and the Blood of the glorified, not the crucified Christ. This is a mystical presentation of the doctrine, and perhaps a stronger emphasis needs to be laid upon the idea of 'blood' as life surrendered *in death*. Bishop Hicks' treatment also suffers from the overshadowing of the Pauline teaching concerning the experience of sharing in the power of Christ's self-offering upon the Cross. But undoubtedly his book makes a vital contribution to our apprehension of the doctrine of the Atonement.

9. *G. Aulén (Christus Victor,* 1931). An important Swedish theologian, Aulén vigorously supports what he calls the 'Classic' doctrine of the Atonement, which represents the Cross as the victory of Christ over sin, evil, death, and Satan, and has strong affinities with the 'Ransom Theory' described at the outset. This book made a great impression in Great Britain,[1] and certainly in all that it asserts it is of the greatest value. It brings home to us the values of that view which prevailed so long in the Church, and which has a new importance to-day when so much tends to suggest man's subjection to evil powers and his apparent insignificance in the conflict. It cannot, I think, be regarded as an adequate account of the doctrine, since it tends to ignore other aspects of it presented in the sayings of Jesus and the New Testament generally and emphasized by other theologians of our time. Nevertheless, in the proclamation of a victorious Christ triumphant over evil and sin it strikes a clarion note needed in modern theology.

10. *Emil Brunner (The Mediator,* Eng. tr. 1934). This monumental work is not easy to read rapidly because of the spiral character of Brunner's argument and the uncompromising emphasis he lays upon the immediate

[1] Cf. S. Cave, *The Doctrine of the Work of Christ.*

point under discussion. Great thoughts are hurled at the reader and qualifications appear to be disdained. There can be no doubt, however, that it is a work to be read and pondered frequently.

Brunner denies that the sinner can ever repent in proportion to his sin and affirms that 'there are no human conditions in which we have a right to expect that God will forgive us as a matter of course'.[1] His views on repentance recall those of Campbell and Moberly when he writes, 'If we could repent as we should no atonement would be needed, for then repentance would be atonement',[2] and again, 'Only "in Christ", and indeed in the Cross of Christ, can we really repent'.[3]

His views on the divine judgement have an austere sound when he describes it as not educative and paternal, but rather as 'the punishment of a sovereign inflicted on a rebellious subject'.[4] At the same time he holds that mercy and justice are not at variance. 'The Cross', he says, 'is the only possible way in which the absolute holiness and the absolute mercy of God are revealed together.'[5]

An important aspect of his discussion is the fact that he holds that what he calls the 'ritual idea' is also necessary in order to set forth the meaning of the Cross, since the death of Christ is an expiatory sacrifice. In forceful words he writes:

'God alone can make this sacrifice. He alone can expiate, can "cover" guilt as though it had never been; He alone can stop up the hole, fill up the trench; for there is something infinite about sin.'[6]

His submission is that God reconciles Himself in Christ the Mediator. In a striking phrase he described man's position as one of 'confident despair'. Instead of charac-

[1] *Op. cit.*, 447.   [2] *Op. cit.*, 534.   [3] *Op. cit.*, *ibid.*
[4] *Op. cit.*, 464.   [5] *Op. cit.*, 472.   [6] *Op. cit.*, 482.

terizing Brunner's views further it will be best to conclude this summary account by a particularly moving passage in which he speaks of man's dependence upon Christ:

'All these inner moods and feelings, as they rise and fall, toss like the waves of the sea over an immovable sheet of rock, upon which these words are clearly inscribed: "I belong to Christ, in spite of everything, in spite of my moods and feelings, in spite of all my experience of my impotence, even in the sphere of faith. I belong to Christ, not because *I* believe in Him, but because of what Christ has said, through the Word which God has spoken to me in Him, the Mediator".'[1]

III. TENDENCIES OF THE PERIOD

Without discussing in detail the works I have described and important books of later date I wish, in conclusion, to summarize what seem to me to be the tendencies of the period.

1. The tendency to reject theories of substitutionary punishment is clearly marked.

2. But along with this rejection an earnest desire is manifest to meet the problems arising out of the divine judgement which rests upon sin. In some cases there is an unwillingness to use in any sense the word 'penal', but in notable cases the word is still used to describe the penal conditions which Christ accepted in His identification with sinful men. Christ's sufferings, it is felt, had a penal character, but were not in themselves a direct punishment which He endured.

3. A close connexion is recognized between Christ Himself and sinners, in virtue of which He 'bore' the sins of men. His relation to them is that of a representative, a kinsman, a 'high priest'. The fact that He speaks for men, as an intercessor, is recognized even by

[1] *Op. cit.*, 526.

those theologians who hesitate to speak of His ministry as 'the sacrifice of supreme penitence'.

4. An equally marked tendency is to affirm a close relationship between Christ and His deed, and the faith of the believer, and to find this faith relationship in union with Christ, sacramental communion, and worship.

5. A growing tendency can be seen to interpret the Cross in terms of sacrifice understood in the light of Old Testament teaching.

TOWARDS A MODERN STATEMENT
OF THE DOCTRINE

In this final lecture I propose to attempt to give a modern presentation of the doctrine of the Atonement. I fully recognise the difficulty of this undertaking, and I do not profess to be able to do more than to indicate how I view the doctrine after many years of study and reflection. For the reasons stated in the Preface to these lectures, my statement is based on New Testament teaching, since Scripture is the touchstone of faith. I also believe it to be in harmony with the mind of the Church, as reflected in her teaching and worship, and, I trust, with that illumination of the Spirit which is given to those who seek it.

I begin by defining the character of the doctrine. The Atonement is the work of God in Christ for man's salvation and renewal. It is an attempt to explain, so far as an explanation is possible, how man is delivered from his pride and his overweening confidence in himself and is brought into a true and abiding fellowship with God, and so is empowered to fulfil his divine destiny as an individual and as a member of society.

This end man cannot fulfil by any power or effort of his own. Only by the act of God in Christ can he attain to communion with God and to the knowledge of life in its fulness.

In its nature and scope, the Atonement is both deliverance and attainment. It concerns man's sin and his blessedness; and it cannot be the one without being at the same time the other. It is the doctrine which tells how God delivers him from the predicament in which he finds himself and how He makes it possible for him to know the joy of eternal life, that is, of life in the fulness of its meaning.

The best word to describe the character of this divine purpose is, I believe, reconciliation. This word has the advantage of including all that is meant by 'redemption' and 'forgiveness', with the added merit of describing the restoration of personal relations with God, broken by sin, and their permanent security in an ever-growing fellowship of love. St. Paul has given classic expression to this doctrine when he writes, 'In Christ God was reconciling the world to himself' (2 Cor. v. 19).

It is important at the outset to distinguish two aspects of the doctrine which can be separated in thought, but not without grave loss in practice. These are, as we saw in considering the teaching of St. Paul, (*a*) the saving deed of Christ, and (*b*) the appropriation of His work by faith, both individual and communal. These two *together* constitute the Atonement. Neither is complete in itself. This fact explains why many statements of the doctrine seem artificial and remote like a transaction completed outside of, and apart from, ourselves. It is as if a living tissue were taken from the body and placed upon a slide for purposes of observation. No longer an organ functioning within a living whole, it appears to be inert and dead. Only when the saving deed of Christ is appropriated by the response of faith is it truly seen, for it is then fulfilling the purpose it was meant to serve. Nevertheless, for theological thinking this separation is necessary. Only so can we perceive the true nature of the saving deed and the response of faith, and the dangers of separation can be avoided if we are aware of them.

Certainly both are necessary to the doctrine. We need an objective deed which in its sublimity stands apart from us, something which is there whether we accept it or not, something which is true whether we believe or whether we reject it, a stark irremovable reality which exists in its own right and which owes nothing to ourselves by way of creation or action. Such a reality is the saving deed of God in Christ. But we need also a believing response if this deed is to become effective in our relationships with God. This response is faith union with Christ. The exercise of faith does not mean that by it man himself effects his reconciliation with God, for, while faith is spiritual venture, it is also, as I shall show, the gift of God to us. Faith is the spiritual appropriation of Christ's saving deed. In consequence, atonement is both accomplished *for us* and wrought *in us*.

I. THE SAVING DEED OF CHRIST

What is it, then, that Christ has done for us? How shall we describe His saving deed? What is the meaning of the Cross?

I preface my answer by insisting that, throughout, it is Christ as the Son of God who became man of whom I am speaking, and that, as explained in the first lecture, I interpret His saving deed both as an event in time and also as a present and continuous ministry on high. If I say 'on high', this is because without this familiar language we cannot make this ministry luminous in our thinking.

I wish also to insist that the possibility of this ministry depends upon the closeness of His relationship to mankind. Without this relationship it is not conceivable. That is why in various ways the New Testament presents Christ as the Son of Man, the Suffering Servant, and the Second Adam.

G

I begin by reminding you of three characteristic aspects of Christ's saving deed. (*a*) First, it is *vicarious*; it is wrought on behalf of men. On this point, if we accept New Testament teaching, there is no room for doubt. Every strand of its teaching reveals the primitive belief that Christ died 'for us'. This statement, however, requires further definition, since it raises the question, 'In what sense did He die for us?' (*b*) Secondly, the deed of Christ is *representative*; it is accomplished in our name. As the Son of Man He is head of the community for which He suffers and dies. This conviction is expressed in New Testament language when He is said to give Himself 'a ransom for many' (Mk. x. 45) and when His out-poured life is described as 'my blood of the covenant, which is shed for many' (Mk. xiv. 24). The belief that He acts in the name of men is taught by St. Paul (2 Cor. v. 21), St. Peter (ii. 24), St. John (i. 29, I Jn. ii. 1f.), and the writer of Hebrews (ix. 24). It is implicit in the use of such names as 'high priest', 'surety', 'mediator', 'Lamb of God', and 'Advocate with the Father'. I believe that this teaching is a valid description of Christ's saving deed. I think it is better to describe His ministry as 'representative' rather than 'substitutionary', although I recognise that it is substitutionary in the sense that it is a service which we are quite unable to accomplish ourselves.

(*c*) Thirdly, the saving deed is *sacrificial*; it is an act of self-offering on our behalf. This again is New Testament teaching. Indeed, there is no aspect of Christ's deed which is so widely attested in the New Testament. Especially notable in I Peter and the Apocalypse, sacrificial language concerning 'the blood' of Christ is found in the Pauline and Pastoral Epistles, in the Johannine writings, and on a remarkable scale in the Epistle to the Hebrews. Analogies are traced in the Old

Testament sacrifices, ideas like 'cleansing', 'washing', and 'redeeming' are used, and, without their pagan associations, terms like 'expiatory' (Rom. iii. 25) and 'expiation' (1 Jn. ii. 2) appear. This teaching, I believe, is of permanent value. Christian thought has not been mistaken in speaking of Christ's self-offering as 'the One Sacrifice' for the sin of the world. Few theologians who recognize the authority of Scripture would deny this claim. The point where differences of opinion arise, and where further explanation is needed, is the character of the One Sacrifice and the ideas which it implies.

Let me say at once that, in speaking of Christ's deed as a sacrifice, I do not mean that His death 'propitiates' the Father, so that, in consequence of it, He becomes gracious to sinners and forgives their sins. This conception is pagan. It also implies division within the Godhead, in that the compassionate Son is set over against the just and holy Father. The true presupposition of the doctrine of the Atonement is the fact that God is love and that in the work of reconciliation Father, Son, and Holy Spirit are at one. Further, I do not think it necessary to select any one of the Old Testament sacrifices, as for example the sin-offering, as the type which Christ's Sacrifice fulfils. In His self-offering there are elements only faintly represented in the Old Testament rites and aspects not found in them at all. It is the *basic pattern* in these sacrifices which serves as a vehicle for the New Testament doctrine—*the idea of a representative offering with which the worshipper identifies himself, so that it becomes the means of his approach when in penitence he 'draws near' to God*. And it has this further advantage: it finds room both for the idea of Christ's self-offering and also for the approach of faith by which His deed is appropriated. In short, the sacrificial concept is a fitting mould into which

G2

the seething metal of the doctrine can be poured. Never-theless, so rich is the ministry of Christ that the mould is first filled and then broken. This is the fate of every vehicle by which we attempt to convey the truth of the Atonement. The value of the sacrificial pattern, in my submission, is that it is richer and more adequate than any other. It is not too much to claim that the work of Christ is vicarious because it is representative, and repre-sentative because it is sacrificial.

Thus far I have been speaking of the *character* of Christ's saving deed. What is its *content*? What is it that Christ does for us? With a full recognition that no answers to this question can be complete I propose to put forward four points which seem to me to be of essential importance. First, the saving deed of Christ is the supreme revelation of the love of God; secondly, it is an act of obedience to His sovereign will; thirdly, it is an act of submission, in the name of sinners, to the judge-ment of God upon sin; fourthly, it is a ministry of inter-cession in which the Son of God voices the penitence of humanity and makes Himself the vehicle of man's approach to God.[1]

1. *First, the saving deed of Christ is the supreme revelation of the love of God for men.* No Christian will deny this truth. For the non-Christian the statement is a challenge to decision, dependent upon his belief in God and his perception of the revelation. The classical statements in Scripture are Rom. v. 8 and Jn. iii. 16, and in the history of doctrine such words as those of Abelard: 'This was the singular grace shown to us, through which He more abundantly bound us to Himself by love, so that, set on

---

[1] It will be of advantage to consider these points, not only those we readily accept, but those which prove difficult and which we are disposed to reject. Progress in theological thinking consists in pondering deeply views which challenge us.

fire as we are by so great a benefit from Divine grace, true charity should fear nothing at all'. If we cannot say more, let us rejoice to say this to ourselves and to others, until we can no longer forbear to ask, 'But what does this love *do?*'.

2. *Secondly, the saving deed of Christ is an act of obedience to the Father's will.* This truth also is Scriptural, for St. Paul speaks of it when he says that 'through the obedience of the one shall the many be made righteous' (Rom. v. 19), and when also in the sublime Hymn to Christ in Phil. ii. 6–11 the climax of Christ's humiliation is that He became 'obedient even unto death, yea the death of the cross' (Phil. ii. 8). So too when the author of Hebrews says that 'though he was a son', He 'yet learned obedience by the things which he suffered' (Heb. v. 8). This emphasis upon Christ who came 'not to be served, but to serve' (Mk. x. 45) is of particular moment in an age when obedience tends to be identified with servility, when 'we are all masters now' and therefore unhappy. Jesus said, 'Whosoever would become great among you shall be your servant' (Mk. x. 43) and 'Whosoever would be first among you shall be bond-servant of all' (Mk. x. 44). Jesus not only taught this, but embodied it in His life and death. He did not regard equality with God as something to be clutched, but emptied himself, taking the form of a slave (Phil. ii. 6f.).

3. *Thirdly, Christ's saving deed was an act of submission to the judgement of God upon sin.* He identified Himself with sinners and bore the sins of men. The friend of taxgatherers and sinners during His ministry on earth, He could not but share the weight of that divine judgement which rests upon sin as He approached the Cross and felt its shame. This experience is probably the key to those strange words of St. Mark in the story of

Gethsemane, 'And he takes with him Peter and James and John, and began to be greatly amazed, and sore troubled' (Mk. xiv. 33), 'My soul', He said, 'is sorrowful even unto death' (Mk. xiv. 34), and His prayer was, 'Abba, Father, all things are possible unto thee; remove this cup from thee: howbeit not what I will, but what thou wilt' (Mk. xiv. 36).

For upwards of a century[1] most theologians have ceased to speak of this experience of His as one of *vicarious punishment* and many would hesitate to describe it as *penal suffering*. One can understand this hesitation, for the word *'penal'* has unfortunate associations connected with laws and law courts. For this reason it is not a suitable word to be used in preaching. Unfortunately, for purposes of theology, no good alternative has been suggested. We need carefully to consider what it means when it is used of the work of Christ, lest through a natural revulsion of feeling we lose a vital aspect of His saving deed.

Much depends upon whether we believe that the judgement of God rests upon evil and sin and whether we attenuate this belief into the idea of a self-acting law of cause and effect visible in its consequences. Speaking for myself, I do not see how those who believe in the living God can doubt that His judgement rests upon evil doers both individuals and nations, although its existence is not always immediately discerned. *'Mene, mene, tekel, upharsin'*[2] can often be read in the pages of history, and the great dramatists, poets, and novelists, Aeschylus, Shakespeare, Ibsen, Hardy, and Hawthorne, see it clearly. Philosophers and theologians often discuss how far punishment is a deterrent, how far it is disciplinary, and whether it is retributive, frequently with serious

---

[1] See earlier, p. 85.　　[2] Dan. v. 25.

doubts as to its retributive character. On this question I can only say that it is not defensible as a deterrent, and is not likely to be remedial, unless it is recognized as just, and in this sense retributive, but not vindictive. This discussion, however, conceives punishment within the domain of law. Judgement is the reaction of a God of love, a love so deep that evil cannot be ignored, but must be allowed to work itself out in pain and frustration, and must be overcome by grace.

Now it is a fact of experience that the divine judgement upon sin is rarely felt by the wrongdoer until his eyes are opened. Its poignant reality is felt by those who love him, and most of all by those who love him best. The supreme example of this truth is the saving act of Christ who bore the sins of men. So deep was His love that He could do no other. On the Cross, as W. Russell Maltby has said,[1] He betrothed Himself to sinful men, sharing their lot and pledging Himself to their recovery.

4. *Fourthly, the saving deed of Christ issues in a ministry of intercession in which He voices our inarticulate penitence and desire for reconciliation.*

The place of Christ at the right hand of God is affirmed in every part of the New Testament, and by St. Paul (Rom. viii. 34), St. John (I Jn. ii. 1), and the writer of Hebrews (ix. 24) it is represented as one of victory and of intercession. This representation is pictorial and poetic, perhaps the only kind of interpretation by which its truth can be communicated. Its meaning as the sacrifice of penitence is not taught in Scripture, but is the significance found in it by J. McLeod Campbell[2] and R. C. Moberly.[3] As I have taken occasion to point out

---

[1] *The Cross of Christ* (Fellowship Manuals), *Christ and His Cross*, 77f., 94f., 165.
[2] See p. 73f.   [3] See p. 79f.

elsewhere,[1] neither of these theologians had any thought
of suggesting a *substituted* repentance or penitence, but
an offering with which we are increasingly to identify
ourselves in faith. This, in my view, is one of the greatest
insights of modern theology.

It is often claimed that man's repentance is enough.
This claim is frequently sustained by an appeal to the
Parable of the Prodigal Son (Lk. xv. 11–32), where the
prodigal repents and is forthwith forgiven by his father.
To base a theory of the Atonement on the parables is
inadmissible, especially since A. Jülicher's epoch-making
discussion[2] of the parables, in which he shows that the
parable has one main point and one only. The point of
this parable is the picture of the loving father with its
unexpressed claim '*So ist Gott*', '*So is God*',[3] and since the
Cross is not contemplated, beyond that, I think, we
should not go. Moreover, at its best our penitence is
fitful, partial, and individualistic. It needs to expand its
broken wings by resting upon a perfect penitence voiced
by the Son of God, somewhat as our inarticulateness finds
expression in great music and in great poetry.[4] Who
has not found release of spirit in Bach and Beethoven, in
Sibelius and Debussy, and a voice in Shelley and Browning
and Emily Brontë and many others? I remember once
sitting with a friend by a peat fire in Scotland as we tried
to talk of a mutual friend no longer with us. Suddenly
after a silence my friend began to quote Shelley's *Adonais*,

> 'Peace, peace! he is not dead, he doth not sleep—
> He hath awakened from the dream of life—
> 'Tis we, who lost in stormy visions, keep
> With phantoms an unprofitable strife.'

---

[1] See pp. 74, 79, also *Jesus and His Sacrifice*, 309.
[2] *Die Gleichnisreden Jesu* (1899, 2nd ed. 1910).
[3] Cf. J. Jeremias, *The Parables of Jesus* (Eng. tr. 1954), p. 27, 105.
[4] Cf. *Jesus and His Sacrifice*, 315.

Shelley was our mediator who uttered what we could not say. So, but on a grander scale, there is a Mediator on high who voices the silence of the soul. Christ is our daysman in our dealings with God.

All that I have said thus far is doubtless inadequate as an account of Christ's saving deed. But when the utmost has been said, we have not yet apprehended the Atonement. To our best words there must be added some account of faith by which Christ's work is made the organ of our approach to God.

II. THE RESPONSE OF FAITH

What is faith? This is a question we cannot ask too often or reflect upon too much. Christian faith, I shall submit, is (a) dependence upon Christ, (b) it is the gift of God, (c) it is communal, (d) it is shaped by its object, Christ, and (e) it is expressed in life.

1. *First, faith is dependence upon Christ,* trust in Him with complete abandon of spirit. Just as a gull, driven by the wind, comes to rest upon the shelving rock, so the soul drops its wings and rests in the breast of God.

> 'Jesu, Lover of my soul,
> Let me to Thy bosom fly.'

2. *Further, while personal, faith is also communal.* It is shaped and inspired by Scripture, by Christian teaching, by worship, and by our knowledge of the faith of others. Doubtless, faith can be found in loneliness; yet even the loneliness is full of voices, of hands that reach out to us, and memories that speak. Distinctive as it was, St. Paul's faith in Christ was upborne by the faith of his fathers in the promises of God and by the glowing confidence of the primitive Jerusalem community. Our debt to the worship of the Church cannot be assessed. Hymns,

rites, and confessions enrich our faith. In particular, the
sacrament of the Lord's Supper is an act of communion
with Christ and a pleading of His Sacrifice. He Himself
gave it this significance, when He said of the bread,
'Take. This is my body (that is, myself)', and of the
cup, 'This is my blood of the covenant, which is shed for
many' (Mk. xiv. 22, 24).

3. *Again, while faith is spiritual venture, it is also the
gift of God.* At first we may not recognize this fact. So
much is the venture our own that it appears to be wholly
ours. Further knowledge reveals that the impulse to
believe came to us from God. He made it possible; He
evoked it and called it into being. That is why, on
reflection, our faith seems miraculous, almost as if we had
nothing to do with it at all. This truth is expressed by
the Johannine Christ in the words, 'No man can come
to me, except the Father which sent me *draw him*' (Jn.
vi. 44). Election is a New Testament concept. God
calls all men, but in His own time and in His own way.
This truth throws light upon a perplexing question.
Why is faith so often difficult to ourselves and others?
The cause may be intellectual, but it may also be that
God's hour has not yet struck. But at His time the bell
strikes, often in His mercy again and again. Then, if
we respond, faith is instinctive. Our restless heart finds
rest in Him. 'By grace have you been saved through
faith', wrote St. Paul, 'and that not of yourselves: it is
the gift of God: not of works, that no man should glory'
(Eph. ii. 8f.).

4. *Once more, faith gains its substance through Christ.*
Here we come to the heart of the matter. Faith is not a
purely subjective response; it is objectively controlled by
the fact of Christ. Its character is determined by what
He is and by what He has done. That is why, when

the Apostle says that he lives in faith, he immediately defines it as 'the faith which is in the Son of God, who loved me, and gave himself up for me' (Gal. ii. 20). Christ makes it what it is. And He does this because He is Christ.

We shall see this truth more clearly if we will consider how faith is affected by Christ's nature and deed. Were He no more than a Galilean saint, our attitude to Him would be one of veneration. If He were only a great ethical teacher, our faith in Him would be admiration and respect for the truths which He uttered, a lovely thing, but only a flower in the teeth of a gale. But, if it be true, that in Christ God has made Himself known, that for us men and our salvation, the Word became flesh, that the Son of God loved us and gave Himself for us, that He conquered sin and death, and ever lives to make intercession for us; then faith will be a flaming fire, kindling the mind, engaging the heart, making resolute the will, filling the whole personality with love for God and therefore with love for men. And it will be all this, not because we are temperamentally so inclined, but because the One in whom our faith rests constitutes it and makes it what it becomes.

This view of faith explains a curious fact of religious history. Many of the greatest leaders of the thought and life of the Church have been men with a rationalistic bent of mind. St. Augustine, St. Thomas Aquinas, John Calvin, Bishop Butler, John Wesley, and John H. Newman will serve as examples. These men loved and deeply honoured reason. Whence, then, came their faith? The explanation can only be that faith was wrought in them, not merely effected by them; they were products as well as exemplars of faith. And from this consideration we may infer that men can be sceptics by nature and believers by grace, since faith is begotten, founded, and integrated by Him on whom it rests. Christ makes that for which He asks.

5. *Lastly, faith is organically connected with life.* The Christian ethic is the overflow of life in Christ. It is a result rather than a goal, something that happens rather than something that is sought. It is this because we cannot trust in Christ without loving the things which He loves and embodies. Here is the secret of the saints. They do not strike us as men who are balancing a caber or otherwise engaged in a desperate enterprise, but as men with a certain gaiety of spirit. This was certainly true of St. Francis. And in our own measure it is given to us ordinary Christians to have some knowledge of these things. We are honest, not because honesty is the best policy, but because in Christ honesty is the law of our mind; truthful, not because lying is evil, but because He is the truth; loving, not because love is the queen of the virtues, but because in fellowship with Him love is life. We care for social morality because He came that we may have life and may have it abundantly. Throughout, Christian morality is conditioned by faith in Christ. 'Works' are the flowers of faith.

Such, then, is faith. It remains for me to show how faith enables us to appropriate the blessings of Christ's saving deed, so that He becomes the means of our reconciliation with God.

III. FAITH AS THE APPROPRIATION OF CHRIST'S SAVING DEED

On this question two important things need to be said.

1. The simplest exercise of faith is enough to bring us into a saving relationship with Christ. I have attempted to describe faith in all the wealth of its range.

It would be wrong, however, to suggest that only when faith is at the richest stage of its growth is reconciliation possible. Such a claim would lead to a subtle form of justification by works by presenting salvation as something to be earned. The truth is that the simplest form of faith in Christ contains within itself the germ and the potency of its fullest development. That is why the simplest appeal of the evangelist may prove to be the genuine beginning of the Christian experience. The best illustration of this truth is the story of the Philippian jailer. 'Sirs', he cried, 'what must I do to be saved?' (Ac. xvi. 30). 'Believe on the Lord Jesus, and thou shalt be saved', was the immediate reply of Paul and Silas. To this statement it needs to be added that such faith is but a beginning. All the growth of faith through devotion and worship remains, and especially because Christ's saving deed issues in the activity of a continuous ministry.

2. The second thing to be said is that reconciliation does not depend on a full theological grasp of Christ's atoning work. We need at all times to remember that the Church has never defined the work of Christ as she has done in the case of His person in the Apostles' and Nicene Creeds. The only reference to Christ's death is the phrase 'crucified under Pontius Pilate'. Of course, taken too literally, this statement of the case is misleading, since in her hymns and her worship, and, above all, in her dependence upon Scripture as the rule of faith, a rich theology is implied. Nevertheless, this theology is not a prerequisite of reconciliation. We are saved as and when we believe in Christ. Herein is seen the peculiar value of the Fourth Gospel, for, as we have seen, this Gospel brings the person and the work of Christ into the closest possible connexion, notably when it presents His death as His glorifying and His victory over evil. Still more

emphatic is the statement of the First Epistle, 'And *He* is the expiation' (ii. 2), although, it should be remembered, this passage is preceded by the words, 'We have an advocate with the Father, Jesus Christ the righteous' (ii. 1). It is the glory of the Gospel that even ignorant and way-faring men can find peace with God through believing in Christ, without having any theology of the Atonement. The reason for this is that all that He does for our salvation is implicit in Himself. He is the Crucified and Exalted Lord, and in Him is our peace.

While, however, simple faith in Christ, without theological elaboration, can be justified, it is wrong to conclude that the deeper issues can be left to theologians. In this matter the Christian believer has great interests at stake. It must surely be true that experience will have a deeper and a richer content if what Christ did, and still does, is accepted and appropriated by faith. The Atonement cannot be left in the background of our religion. With the Incarnation it must be its centre and governing motive.

How, then, we ask, does faith take hold of Christ's benefits?

(*a*) Faith's response to the death of Christ as the supreme revelation of the love of God is immediate and complete. An answering flame of love is kindled by it in the heart, which can never die down or fail, especially if we see, even in part, what Christ's love enabled Him to endure and do.

(*b*) Again, faith accepts Christ's willing obedience to death as the norm of Christian living. Christ's words, spoken and embodied in His humiliation, ring in our ears: 'You know that they which are accounted to rule over the Gentiles lord it over them; and their great ones exercise authority over them. But it is not so among you' (Mk. x. 42f.). To serve, and not to count the cost, becomes the Christian imperative.

(*c*) Further, faith sees that, because Christ submitted Himself to that judgement of God upon evil and sin, He is in truth the Lamb of God who takes away the sin of the world. Faith rests in Him as such. It knows that, in our reconciliation with God, eternal and moral values have not been flouted or ignored. Awed by the fact of divine sin-bearing, it learns that to suffer with Christ in this saving ministry is the lot and privilege of all who love Him.

(*d*) Lastly, faith enters into, and receives, all the meaning of Christ's ministry on high. With His offering of sorrow and penitence it identifies itself, making it the focal point of all penitence, the world anthem in which all human voices are merged. Sacramental communion is a communal expression of faith conditioned by the use of symbols of Christ's appointing. It is not fundamentally different from, and is certainly not an alternative to, personal faith in Christ. The growing interest in the Lord's Supper in the theology of our time and in the life of the Church is due to a Biblical impulse and to a sounder doctrine of the Church as a living society marked by devotion to the Exalted Lord. Its Biblical foundations are due to a closer study of the sacred meal in Old Testament religion, of prophetic symbolism, and above all of Christ's words and acts in the New Testament narratives of institution (Mk. xiv. 21–5, Lk. xxii. 14–20, Mt. xxvi. 20–9) and the teaching of St. Paul (I Cor. x. 16–21, xi. 23–5). In the Lord's Supper, with angels and archangels and the whole company in heaven, the believer is brought into communion with Christ, pleads His Sacrifice, and shares in the power of His saving ministry. Methodists[1] should have no doubts about the

---

[1] Methodists are mentioned because the Lectures were delivered in a University of Methodist foundation. The points made are included since they are of much wider application.

value of this teaching if they are familiar with the story of their origins, for it is a delusion to think that the Wesleys receded from their earlier emphasis upon the value of the Lord's Supper. On the contrary, they maintained it until the end. As long as they were permitted they led their followers in hundreds to the altars of the Church of England. Their *Hymns on the Lord's Supper*, 161 in number, were republished at least ten times and were prefaced by Dr. Brevint's essay on 'The Christian Sacrament and Sacrifice'. The Societies in London communicated every Sunday and John Wesley himself every four or five days until the time of his death. And the Wesleys have left to us the legacy of some of their greatest hymns in 'Victim Divine, Thy grace we claim', 'Entered the Holy Place above', and 'Lamb of God, whose dying Love'. There can be no doubt that in their sacramental worship they entered the very gates of heaven and knew the power of Christ's saving ministry on high.

This experience we need to recover. It may be granted that rites are meaningless if they are isolated from spiritual realities. The important thing is the devotion they make possible and the significance which Christ gives to them. Perhaps our greatest need to-day, if we would rise above the poverty of much of our worship, is to experience once more the wonder of reliance upon Christ's ceaseless saving ministry, which is the true centre of Christian devotion and the abiding source of Christian living.

Such, then, is the account of the meaning of the Atonement which I present to you for your consideration as a faith for to-day. It may be called the Sacrificial Theory. Like all theories, it sees the truth concerning God's reconciliation of the world through Christ by way of images, and therefore in part, but I know of none which brings us so near to the veil of the Holy of Holies.

INDEX OF SCRIPTURE QUOTATIONS

Genesis
  xiv. 18–20   52
  xv. 6   36

Leviticus
  xvi.   55

Deuteronomy
  vi. 21   6

Psalms
  ii. 7   13
  l. 13–15   21
  lxix. 9   46
  cx. 1   22, 58
  cx. 4   52

Isaiah
  viii. 3   44n
  xx. 2   44n
  xl. 1 f   6
  xlii. 1   13
  xlv. 15   6
  xlviii. 20   6
  liii.   14, 19, 81
  liii. 1   64n
  liii. 4 f   20
  liii. 11   20
  liii. 12   16, 20

Jeremiah
  vii. 21–23   21
  xix. 10   44n
  xxviii. 10   44n

Ezekiel
  iv. 3   44n

Daniel
  v. 25   94
  vii. 13   18

Hosea
  vi. 2   17

Amos
  v. 25 f   21

Jonah
  iv. 5   42

Micah
  vi. 7 f   21

Matthew
  x. 32   22
  xx. 19   14
  xxvi. 20–29   103

Mark
  i. 11   13
  ii. 1–iii. 6   13
  ii. 20   13
  iii. 6   14
  vi. 17–29   13
  vii. 1–23   14
  viii. 11–13   14
  viii. 31   13, 14 f
  viii. 32   19
  viii. 34   41
  viii. 38   18, 22
  ix. 12   14 f
  ix. 31   14 f
  x. 32   19
  x. 33 f   14 f
  x. 38   18
  x. 39   41
  x. 42 f   102
  x. 43   93
  x. 44   93
  x. 45   14 f, 16, 20 f, 90, 93
  xii. 35–37   23
  xiv. 21–25   22, 103
  xiv. 22   21, 44n, 98
  xiv. 24   14 f, 16 f, 21 f, 44n, 90, 98
  xiv. 25   22

Mark, *continued*

xiv. 33	20, 94
xiv. 34	94
xiv. 36	20, 94
xiv. 62	18
xv. 25	1
xv. 34	20
xv. 37	68
xv. 46	4

Luke

xi. 47	13
xii. 8	22
xv. 11–32	96
xv. 20	38
xvii. 25	14 f
xviii. 9–14	38
xxii. 14–20	103
xxii. 14–18	22
xxii. 15	18
xxii. 16	22
xxii. 19 b	23
xxii. 37	20
xxii. 40	41
xxii. 46	68

John

i. 14	60, 64
i. 29	16, 63, 90
ii. 4	62
iii. 14	62
iii. 15	63
iii. 16	7, 62 f, 69, 92
vi. 53–56	63
vi. 44	98
vii. 6	62
vii. 30	62
x. 11	63
x. 17	62
xi. 33	65
xi. 38	65
xi. 50	63
xii. 23	62, 65
xii. 24	63
xii. 27	67
xii. 31	65
xii. 32	8, 65

xii. 38	64n
xiii. 31 f	65
xiv.	60
xiv. 30	65
xv. 1–10	63
xv. 13	63
xvi. 7	65
xvi. 11	65
xvii. 1	62
xvii. 19	63
xviii. 6	67
xviii. 11	67
xviii. 21	67
xviii. 22	67
xviii. 37	67
xix. 11	67
xix. 15	67
xix. 22	68
xix. 30	68
xx. 29	68
xx. 31	61, 68

Acts

iii. 13	16
iii. 26	16
iv. 27	16
iv. 30	16
xvi. 30	101
xxi. 11	44n

Romans

i. 16 f	36
iii. 24	38
iii. 25 f	32 f
iii. 25	91
iv. 3	27, 36
iv. 20 f	36
iv. 25	16, 29
v. 1 f	39
v. 1	36
v. 7	30
v. 8	7, 30, 69, 92
v. 9	38 f
v. 10	40
v. 11	39
v. 15	79n
v. 12–21	31

Romans, *continued*

v. 19	93
vi. 2	43
vi. 3	43
vi. 4	43
vi. 5 f	44
vi. 8	41
vi. 11	41
vi. 12	29, 44
vi. 14	29
vi. 23	32
viii. 3	27
viii. 11	44
viii. 32	16
viii. 34	7, 16, 34, 48, 59, 95
viii. 35–39	9
viii. 38 f	28
xii. 1	44, 46
xv. 3	46
xv. 16	34

1 Corinthians

i. 14–17	44
ii. 6	28
ii. 8	28
iii. 21–23	9
iv. 11–13	25
v. 7	33
vi. 20	27
x. 4	26
x. 16–21	103
x. 16	45
xi. 23–25	22, 45, 103
xi. 24	16
xi. 25	33
xi. 26	22, 45
xiii.	46
xv. 3 f	16, 24
xv. 3	29
xv. 45	31

2 Corinthians

v. 14	31
v. 19	9, 30, 40, 88
v. 21	27, 31 f, 90
viii. 9	47
xi. 29	25

Galatians

i. 4	29
ii. 16	36
ii. 20	37, 41, 99
iii. 13	27, 31
iii. 16	26
iii. 19 f	30
iii. 24	36
iv. 4	8, 79n
iv. 9	28
iv. 20	25

Ephesians

i. 7	29
ii. 8 f	98
ii. 8	37
ii. 13	41
ii. 16	40
iii. 17	37
iv. 32	46
v. 2	33
vi. 12	28

Philippians

ii. 5	47
ii. 6–11	16, 46, 93
ii. 6 f	93
ii. 7	79n
ii. 8	93
ii. 17	34
iii. 9 f	41
iii. 13 f	39

Colossians

i. 20	29
i. 24	42
i. 27	41
ii. 7	41
ii. 8	28
ii. 14	29
ii. 15	28

1 Timothy

ii. 5	79n
ii. 6	16

2 Timothy

iv. 6	34

Hebrews

i. 1 f	7
i. 2 f	54
i. 3	7, 58
ii. 9	53n, 54
ii. 17	54, 56
iii. 1	54
iv. 15	54
v. 7 f	54
v. 8	93
vi. 19	51
vi. 20	52, 54
vii. 25	58
viii. 1	58
ix. 9	55
ix. 11 f	55
ix. 11	54
ix. 13 f	55
ix. 14	56
ix. 22	57
ix. 23	51
ix. 24	7, 9, 51, 90, 95
ix. 26	56
ix. 28	16, 53n, 56
x. 1	51
x. 4	57

x. 12	1, 58
x. 31	53
xi. 1	52
xii. 2	26, 58
xii. 29	53
xiii. 14	51
xiii. 20	53n

1 Peter

ii. 22–24	16
ii. 24	90

1 John

i. 7	64
ii. 1 f	7, 49, 90
ii. 1	59, 64, 95, 102
ii. 2	63 f, 91
iii. 5	63 f
iii. 8	66
iii. 16	63
iv. 9	63
iv. 10	63, 70
iv. 14	62
v. 4	66
v. 19	66

Apocalypse

v. 12	9

PRINTED IN GREAT BRITAIN BY ROBERT MACLEHOSE AND CO. LTD
THE UNIVERSITY PRESS, GLASGOW